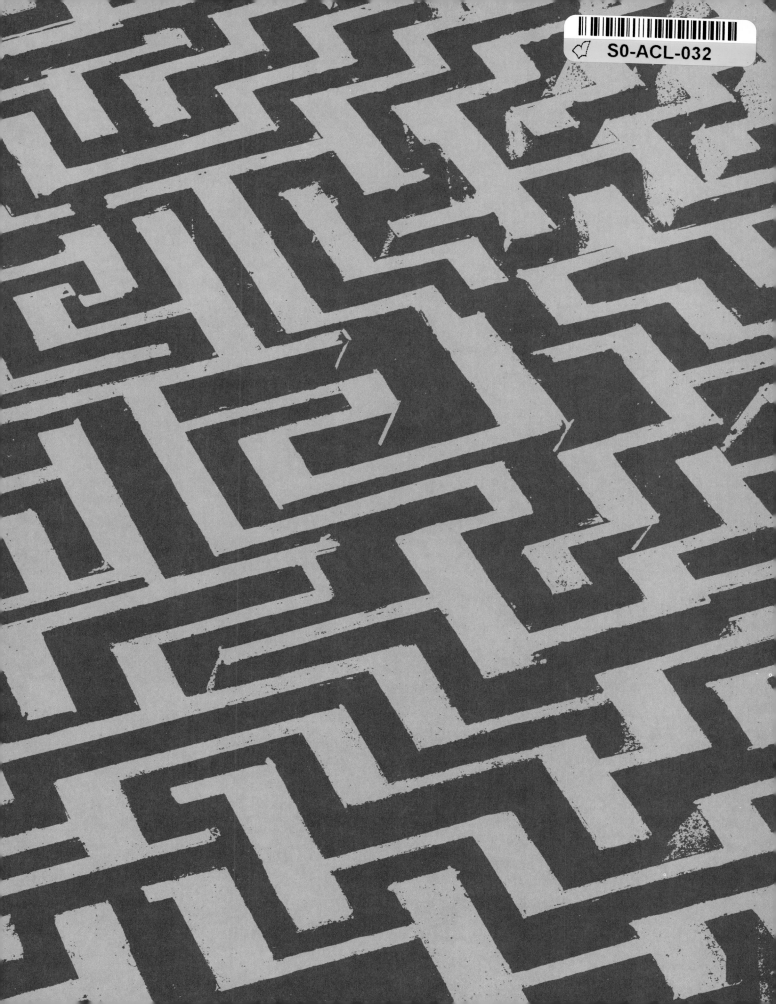

MIND
POWER

QUEST FOR THE UNKNOWN

MIND POWER

THE READER'S DIGEST ASSOCIATION, INC.

Pleasantville, New York/Montreal

Quest for the Unknown
Created, edited, and designed by DK Direct Limited

A DORLING KINDERSLEY BOOK

DK DIRECT LIMITED

Senior Editor Sue Leonard
Editor Nance Fyson
Editorial Research Julie Whitaker

Senior Art Editor Simon Webb
Art Editor Susie Breen
Picture Research Frances Vargo; **Picture Assistant** Sharon Southren

Editorial Director Jonathan Reed; **Design Director** Ed Day
Production Manager Ian Paton

Volume Consultants Douglas Amrine, Brian Inglis
Contributors Reg Grant, Guy Playfair, William George Roll, Frank Smyth, Roy Stemman

Illustrators Roy Flooks, Amanda Ward
Photographers Andrew Atkinson, Howard Bartrop, Martin Eidemak,
Simon Farnhell, Andrew Griffin, Mark Hamilton,
Steve Lyne, Susanna Price, Alex Wilson

Library of Congress Cataloging in Publication Data

Mind power.
        p.   cm. — (Quest for the unknown)
        "A Dorling Kindersley book" — T.p. verso
        Includes index.
        ISBN 0-89577-421-6
        1. Parapsychology—Case studies. I. Reader's Digest Association.
   II.   Series.
   BF1031.M555   1992
   133—dc20   92-4413

Printed in the United States of America

FOREWORD

THE HUMAN MIND HAS ALWAYS BEEN A MYSTERY. The investigation of the unconscious by Freud and the study of brain function by modern scientific techniques have revealed to us far more about the nature of mental activity than our ancestors knew. Even so, that knowledge is rudimentary. We still know little about the full extent of the mind's powers. For this reason, it would be foolish to reject accounts of strange mental abilities simply on the grounds that they seem unbelievable.

Over the years an impressive amount of evidence has built up to show that the mind may in fact have remarkable psychic powers that seem to defy all known natural laws. In this book you will encounter many examples of them, including the mind's apparent ability to communicate directly with other minds and with inanimate objects. You will read of clocks stopping at the time of a person's death, of keys bending under gentle stroking, of murderers being traced by psychic detection, of images being "transmitted" from one person to another, of objects flying across rooms without visible human agency, and many other claimed instances of telepathy, psychokinesis, clairvoyance, precognition, and other psychic phenomena.

MIND POWER will enable you to explore in depth this wide-ranging and fascinating world of the paranormal. In this volume we take care to present both sides of the story. Although the accounts are well documented, we investigate how reliable the evidence really is and whether some of the happenings could have been faked.

In other times and other cultures, psychic powers — which we may all possess to some degree — have been highly valued. But our predominantly rationalist society has consistently dismissed the existence of such abilities. If there is any evidence that they are indeed latent in the human brain, then we should undertake a most urgent quest — to explore the unknown powers of the mind.

— The Editors

CONTENTS

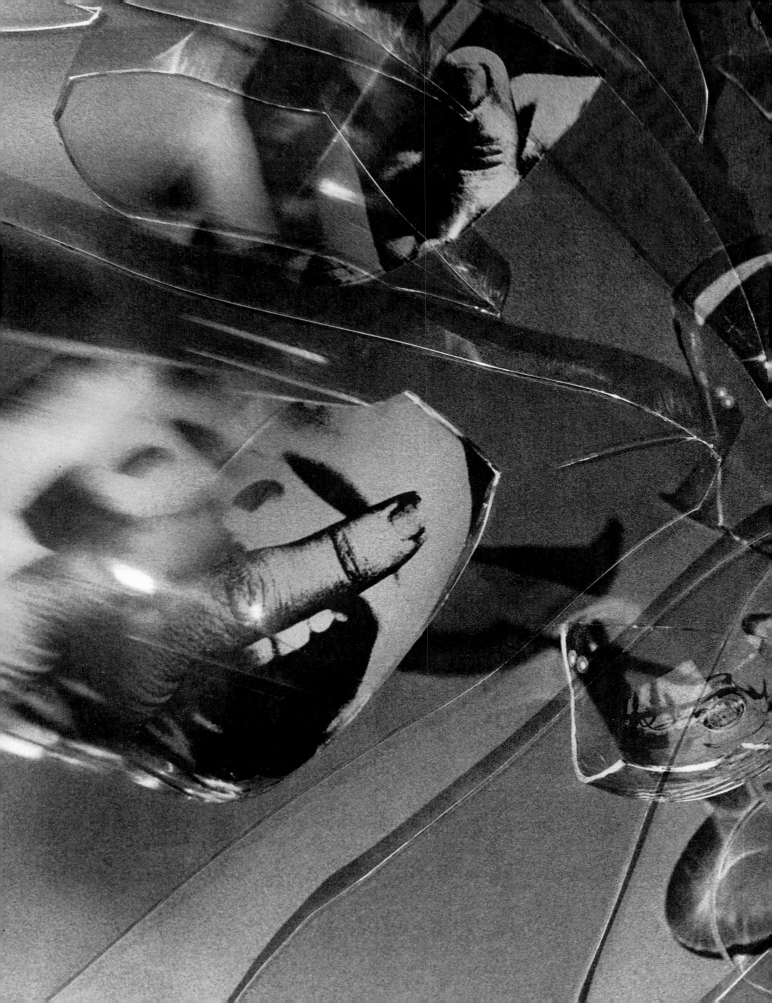

POWER SOURCE

One explanation for paranormal occurrences is that they might be the result of a connection between the known physical world and unknown powers hidden in our own minds. If this theory is correct, could the turbulent thoughts of confused youngsters be responsible for one of the most frightening of unexplained phenomena — the poltergeist?

In March 1984 John and Joan Resch were living in a well-kept house on a quiet street in Columbus, Ohio. John and his wife were an attractive couple, pleasant partners in a union of opposites. He was dark and rather quiet, although friendly when you got to know him. Joan was blond, easy-going, and with a ready smile. The couple had four young foster children living with

Malicious delight

"Poltergeists are 'noisy spirits' whose mischievous and sometimes malicious behavior has been reported from many lands over several centuries. Their chief delight is in throwing things about....It is believed that poltergeists need a medium in order to function. This is usually an adolescent."
International Journal of Parapsychology, No. 6, 1964

Regular breakages

"In poltergeist cases there are often daily movements and breakages of plates, knickknacks, furniture and other movable household effects...."
William G. Roll, The Poltergeist

Unwelcome guests

"A family persecuted by the poltergeist needs help. One common bond uniting poltergeist victims has been their desire to rid themselves of their unwelcomed guest. Few people realize how terrifying the poltergeist can be."
D. Scott Rogo, The Poltergeist Experience

them, as well as their adopted teenage daughter, Tina. Their youngest son, Craig, who was 25 years old, and Pete, the black Labrador dog, also shared their home. In addition John and Joan Resch had four grown-up children who lived away from home.

Over the years Joan Resch had taken care of more than 250 foster children, many of whom had special problems, and her family and friends maintained that she could have won a prize as Foster Mother of the Year. In October 1983, the *Columbus Dispatch* had devoted one of its columns to Joan Resch's fostering care.

Innocuous beginnings

On the evening of Friday, March 2, 1984, the happy family atmosphere of the Resch home was shattered by the onset of increasingly strange and destructive activity. The bizarre events started on a small scale, when the door of the clothes dryer, which stood in a corner of the dining room, suddenly slammed shut, starting up the motor. Every time Joan Resch tried to stop the drying machine by opening the door, the motor would start up again.

Electrical fault

The next day even stranger events occurred: the lights in the house began to switch on by themselves. The family called in the Columbus and Ohio Southern Electric Company to deal with what they assumed must be a power surge, but the maintenance men could find nothing wrong. When the trouble continued, John Resch called in Bruce Claggett, the owner of a local electrical contracting firm. According to Claggett, he tried taping up the light switches, but the lights continued to flash despite the fact that everyone in the house was present and nowhere near the switches.

After three hours, a bewildered and somewhat frightened Claggett left the house. By this time the water faucets in the upstairs tub and sink had begun to turn on by themselves. At first John Resch thought someone had forgotten to turn the faucets off, but they came on again while he watched the stairs to make sure that no one could go into the bathroom without his seeing them.

When candles, lamps, and ornaments began moving, seemingly of their own accord, John Resch called the police. The incidents continued while the police officers were in the house, but they were unable to provide any explanation or solution to the Reschs' problem.

"The eggs were sitting beside the stove and they just started flying."

The source of the unnerving events was not clear, although the incidents appeared to center around 14-year-old Tina. The next morning, according to the story, the family experienced a brief respite when Tina went to church, but when she returned and was getting ready to scramble some eggs, the eggs flew straight up into the air and smashed against the ceiling.

That afternoon, Tina's niece, together with Joyce Beaumont, a family friend, dropped in at the Resch home to see if they could offer assistance. They arrived just in time to witness the eggs shattering on the kitchen ceiling. This is Joyce Beaumont's account of what happened:

❝I was invited to come over on Sunday. I arrived right before two o'clock. Although I had been told what was going on, I didn't really believe any of it. As Tina's niece and I came into the house, I saw some eggs flying out of their container. The eggs were sitting beside the stove and they just started flying.

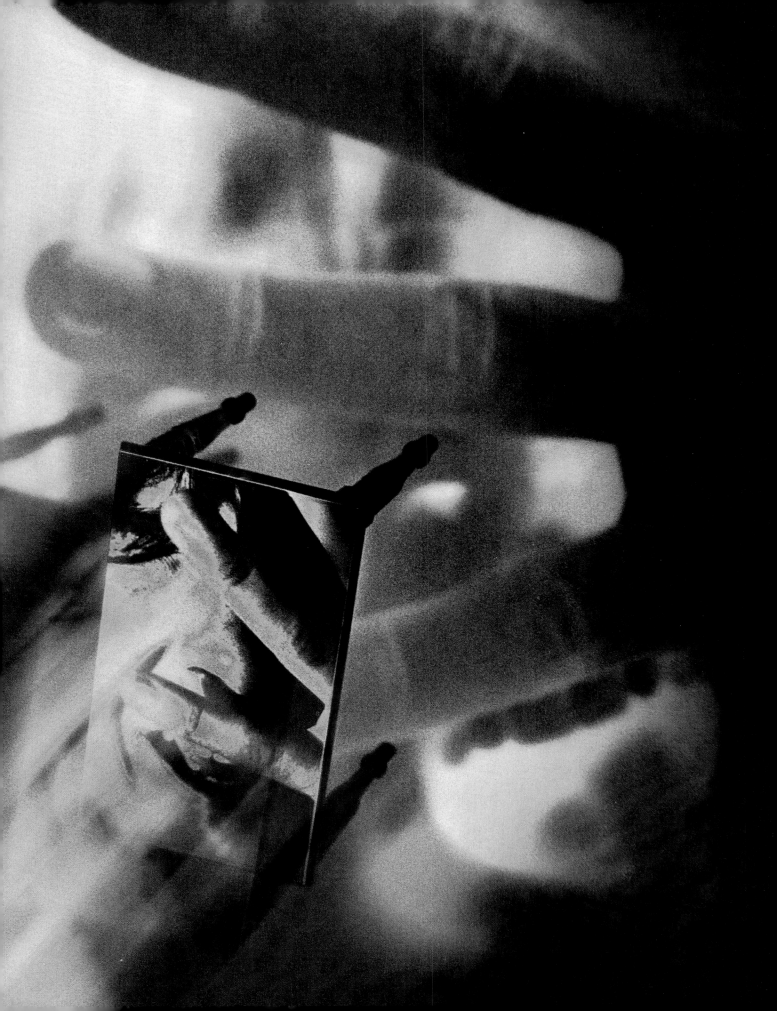

"We went and sat down. At the Reschs' request their Lutheran minister came to see Tina. He prayed with her and then left. Things were calm while the minister was there, but soon after he had gone things started happening. Tina was sitting on the love seat in the family room when a brass candle holder that was standing on the microwave flew and hit her on the back of her head. Another candle that was in a holder on a shelf behind her went flying across the room. Tina could not have reached it. I had been watching her closely because I was beginning to wonder if she was throwing the objects around herself.

> ## "The table flew to the center of the room and when Tina tried to drag it back it fell on top of her, pinning her down."

"And then a clock fell off the shelf, hitting Tina on the back of her head. It just seemed like everything was coming toward her and she was understandably frightened. By this time she was cowering on the floor next to the seat.

"As she was sitting there, the love seat moved two or three inches to the right. When Tina sat on the seat again, it moved another six inches. She leapt to her feet and together we pushed the seat back to its original position.

"Later on I sat with Tina in the dining room as she changed one of the foster children. As I walked out of the dining room and into the hallway a crystal glass landed on the floor in front of me. The hallway light was swinging back and forth. Tina was nowhere near to any of this. Things were becoming really chaotic. Glassware was flying about and we were continually cleaning up the debris that followed. Everything was just happening so fast.

"Tina didn't have to be in a room for things to happen. She was in the family room once when I noticed glasses breaking in the dining room. As I was cleaning up, she came in and said, 'I didn't throw it.' Then she was hit by a tape dispenser that was on the microwave. Everything was hitting the back of her head. It got to the point where she was just holding herself, protecting herself back there on her neck.

Breaking glass

"The breakages continued. A red coffee cup smashed in midair in the kitchen. And the glasses that were sitting on the table kept flying. You could see the liquid start to shake and you thought 'Oh, here it comes,' and the glass would go flying.

"Tina was sitting in one of the chairs in the family room. The phone was on the table next to her and kept crossing her lap. It happened two or three times. She wasn't touching it. Tina was just sitting there with her arms crossed, upset because everyone was blaming her for what was going on.

"I did see her hand just touch a table beside the couch and the table went flying. The stuff that was sitting on the table was constantly flying off and we just kept cleaning up the mess.

"Next, the table moved completely away from the side of the couch. Tina did not touch it at all this time. I know because I was really watching her. The table flew to the center of the room and when Tina tried to drag it back it fell on top of her, pinning her down. She could not get up and she was obviously scared. She was screaming hysterically.

Wanton destruction
"The poltergeist represents the 'dark side of the soul.' Psychic ability can be just as destructive and wicked as it is altruistic."
D. Scott Rogo, The Poltergeist Experience

Incredible explanation
"The idea that the subconscious mind is capable of acting directly upon matter in the real world still seems incredible, although numerous authenticated cases exist in which that seems to be the most likely hypothesis to explain the facts."
Colin Wilson, The Geller Phenomenon

I jumped up, and ran over to pull the table off her. The telephone came flying after me and hit me. I said, 'Enough of this. Someone is gonna get hurt!' I was desperately trying to lift the table. I don't remember pulling the table off until the phone hit me. I had just had enough of it all by that time.

"Then someone called, 'Joyce, come in here.' I went into the living room and found the rocking chair was going back and forth of its own accord. No one was in the room — I don't know who called me. It was all so crazy. I hollered at the chair and told it to stop and it did. I said, 'Okay, I'm leaving.' I left at about three — thirty in the afternoon.

"I thought it was a possession. Tina was not possessed, but it wanted her. Everything came at Tina or anyone who was helping her. **"**

During the hour and a half that Joyce Beaumont had been in the Resch house there had been at least 30 inexplicable incidents — an average of about one every three minutes.

Religious assistance
One of the Reschs' grown sons belonged to the Mormon Church, and he spoke to some elders in his congregation about what was happening at his parents' home. Two elders and a friend of the son volunteered to go to the Resch house to see if they could be

of assistance. That Sunday evening, the Mormons visited Tina and prayed over her. When they laid their hands on Tina's head, all was quiet. But as they left the house, they too apparently saw glasses move in the dining room.

The phenomena continued until Tina went to bed, when things quieted down. By this time the Resch family was at its wits' end. They had called in electricians, policemen, and church leaders, but none of them had been able to determine what it was that was actually causing these disturbances.

> ## While they laid their hands on Tina's head, all was quiet. But as they left the house, they too apparently saw glasses move in the dining room.

Joan Resch then phoned Mike Harden, the journalist at the *Columbus Dispatch* who had written about her fostering five months earlier. Harden went to the house and reported that he saw a variety of bizarre happenings. He saw magazines shoot out from a table, a toy cradle flip two feet off the ground, and a cup of coffee fly through the air. The cup landed first on Tina's lap and then crashed against the fireplace. Harden said that neither Tina nor anyone else seemed to be in a position to cause the strange incidents.

Photographic evidence
Harden next called in a *Dispatch* photographer, who succeeded in snapping pictures of the phone flying across Tina's lap. The next day one of the pictures appeared in newspapers around the world. Harden also called William George Roll at the Psychical

Roll traveled to the Resch home with Kelly Powers, a clinical psychologist. They stayed for six days and talked with everyone who had seen objects flying around, including Joyce Beaumont. Following this visit Dr. Roll has provided us with his conclusions:

"Kelly Powers and I don't think Tina Resch could possibly have caused all the incidents normally. Nor do we think a poltergeist was responsible for them. We suggest that the phenomena were in fact caused by psychokinesis (PK), or mind over matter.

Build-up of pressure

"Tina appeared to be causing the PK involuntarily. Many teenagers have anxiety and anger concerning their parents; this is simply a part of growing up. A few years earlier Tina was subjected to other pressures, especially at school, where the other kids teased her because she wasn't very coordinated. Her teachers finally suggested that she should be taught at home. When all the trouble began in March 1984, Tina had been at home for two years and hadn't left the house much. This could have been part of the problem. She was lashing out at her adoptive parents, probably because of all the pressures she was under.

"It seems that Tina felt restricted and used to dream of a new life. She kept asking Mrs. Resch to give her the name and address of her real mother so she could phone and visit her. Mrs. Resch didn't want to do this as she thought it would just make more problems for Tina. Tina obviously felt extremely resentful about this.

"The PK released and expressed Tina's tension. She was feeling bad about herself and guilty about lashing out at her adoptive parents. Perhaps that's why things kept flying about the house and hitting her.

"I took Tina along to parapsychology laboratories for testing. Although PK events happened there they were much less intense than they had been at Tina's home. Researchers gave Tina psychological tests and even tested her brain waves. The tests showed that there were abnormal brain waves coming from her brain stem. I thought the PK disturbances might be linked to something abnormal in the brain stem, which connects the brain with the spinal column. It seems that instructions from her brain were reaching objects in the environment instead of her body. Maybe that's why she wasn't as coordinated physically as other young people of the same age.

"It seems that instructions from her brain were reaching objects in the environment instead of her body."

Psychic connections

"Tina's case suggests that the human brain may be connected to more than the person's physical body. The brain could be linked to the surrounding environment in ways we don't yet understand. The PK events at the Resch home might be an example of how mind and matter are interwoven. This case certainly indicates that there appear to be intriguing ties between the physical world around us and the

Tense solutions

"Dr John Layard, a Jungian psychologist in Great Britain, was the first to argue that the poltergeist was more the solution to a problem than a problem itself. Layard argued that PK is instrumental in relieving unresolved tension."
D. Scott Rogo, The Poltergeist Experience

Repressed anger

"In most poltergeist cases the agent's repressed anger is usually directed at such emotionally binding targets as parents and guardians."
D. Scott Rogo, The Poltergeist

CHAPTER ONE

MYSTERIES OF THE MIND

To our ancestors it may have seemed obvious that untoward happenings should be blamed on spirits, gods, and devils. But when modern investigators of the paranormal are confronted with a strange event, they tend to seek a human explanation, believing that powers of the mind may be responsible for unexplained phenomena.

The strange powers of the subconscious mind were first identified in the late 19th century by psychologists, most notable among them Sigmund Freud. In the 1880's Freud was studying under the great French neurologist and hypnotist Jean-Martin Charcot, who was fascinated by the apparent influence of the mind over the body, especially in mental patients. For

FAMILY TIES

Dr. Louisa Rhine, wife of pioneering researcher Dr. J. B. Rhine, collected over 12,000 cases of ESP, cases that were submitted to her by ordinary people. The following story is one reported in her book *ESP in Life and Lab* (1967):

"Several years ago, I lived in Virginia. One evening after dark, my wife fell down a long flight of stairs, breaking her left arm above the wrist. The next morning my daughter, living in Colorado, complained to her husband that her left arm pained her awfully and that she could see nothing but her mother. I wrote to them about the accident. My daughter came immediately to Virginia and stayed for a month. I then took her to the train, which left at 10:45 A.M. That evening, while doing the chores around sundown, a wasp stung me in the right eyelid.

Matching symptoms

"The next morning my eye was swollen entirely shut and was very painful. As soon as my daughter arrived home, she reported to my wife as follows: 'Dear Mamma, I had a nice trip home and found the folks all well. But what is the matter with Daddy's eye? My right eye is paining me so I can hardly stand it, and I can see nothing but Daddy. I don't think he is blinded, but his eye is swollen shut. Write me at once.' "

example, Freud noted how female patients diagnosed as suffering from "hysteria" might develop all the symptoms of pregnancy, including the swelling of the abdomen, without being pregnant.

Clearly, he realized, no one would be capable of consciously and deliberately developing the signs of pregnancy. Having worked with various hypnotized patients and having observed Charcot's experiments, Freud then reasoned that there must be some form of unconscious mind, one that had in some ways greater powers than its conscious equivalent. Individuals exerting the power of this unconscious mind would not necessarily be aware of what they were doing. To them the results might seem to be the work of outside forces.

Today many researchers feel that such powers of the mind may be responsible for those aspects of the paranormal that are collectively referred to as psi: extrasensory perception (ESP) and psychokinesis (PK). It was in the 1930's that the term *extrasensory perception* was coined by Dr. J. B. Rhine, who pioneered the statistical study of psychic powers at Duke University, in North Carolina. ESP encompasses telepathy, clairvoyance, precognition, and retrocognition, and refers to the apparent ability of an individual to use any one of these powers to "see" or know about objects or events without the use of the known senses. Dr. Rhine and many other investigators have had no difficulty in accepting the

> **Powers of the mind may be responsible for those aspects of the paranormal that are collectively referred to as psi.**

Paranormal sign
Psi is the 23rd letter of the Greek alphabet and has been used since the late 1940's to represent parapsychological mind powers, including the various aspects of ESP and PK.

possibility that ESP might exist, not as a manifestation of the supernatural, but simply as a function of the brain that science at the present time is not able to explain.

One standard method of testing for the existence of ESP is to place a picture of an object in a sealed envelope and then ask a subject to attempt to produce a drawing to match it. This is a task that some people who claim psychic powers seem to be able to perform often.

In the case of a correctly identified picture in a sealed envelope, however, if special sensory powers exist, it is impossible to tell whether the psychic seer is able somehow to perceive the hidden object directly, through clairvoyance, or whether he or she is in fact using telepathy to read the mind of the person who put the picture into the envelope originally.

Many reported paranormal phenomena might be explained by the existence of a special psychic power that the unconscious mind produces only under extreme circumstances. For example, there are few circumstances more crucial than approaching death, and this unique moment is especially associated with paranormal phenomena. The out-of-body experiences often reported by people near death might represent a sudden intensification of ESP — allowing the dying person to "see" objects and people well out of range of the normal senses. Similarly, it has been suggested that the appearance of a person's ghost to a close relative or friend at the moment of death might be a form of telepathic communication — a projection from the dying person's mind to another mind with which it feels especially in tune.

Other special powers that have been the subject of research are direct knowledge of the future (precognition) and the past (retrocognition), and the ability to control objects by the power of the mind without physical contact (psychokinesis). Some individuals appear to have demonstrated psychokinetic ability under laboratory conditions, where, with great effort, they have appeared capable of moving a

---

The most remarkable reported effects of psychokinesis seem to come not from conscious effort but from the unconscious mind.

---

small object a few inches. Yet perhaps conscious efforts are beside the point. For the most remarkable reported effects of psychokinesis seem to come not from conscious effort but from the unconscious mind.

Psychic disturbances

It is now believed by many researchers that the extraordinary range of effects attributed to "poltergeists" are really a form of psychokinesis caused by an emotionally disturbed individual. The person responsible, the theory suggests, is not consciously making objects fly through the air, or bursting light bulbs, or affecting electric current. It is the disturbed unconscious mind that is doing the damage — and with a force that the conscious mind cannot match.

Can this power of the unconscious mind, if it truly exists, be deliberately harnessed? Since psychic abilities seem to flourish in extreme states, they might be encouraged by creating conditions that are disorienting for the normal conscious mind. Experiments have shown, for example, that sensory deprivation — closing off an individual from sight, sound, and even touch — appears to increase psychic powers. Hypnosis is another reported technique

for releasing the powers of the mind, inducing a state of receptivity to suggestion that makes the hypnotized subject capable of remarkable feats of memory or endurance, or gives them exceptional control over their bodies. And many types of mystics, from medicine men to mediums, have used special rituals or various mind altering intoxicants to induce trance states in order to enhance their psychic abilities.

Nowadays we are familiar with the use of meditation to induce relaxation. Hospitals in the United States are also encouraging patients to use their mental powers on biofeedback techniques to regulate their heart rates or brain wave patterns. Thus it is perhaps not beyond the realm of possibility to suggest that, in the not too distant future, there might be similar developments in the exploitation of mind power, for long-distance perception, communication between individuals, or the control of objects.

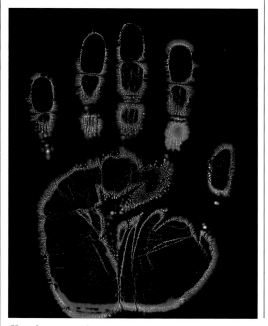

Hand to mouth
Despite the appearance of light in these Kirlian photographs of lips and a hand, no external light source is used with this photographic method. Light is emitted as a result of the interaction between the subject and an applied electrical field, and this produces the stunning images that appear on film.

KIRLIAN PHOTOGRAPHY
In the 1940's researchers at the University of Leningrad discovered that all living creatures are surrounded by a faint electrostatic field called an "electrical aura," which is constantly changing.

At about the same time the Russian husband-and-wife team of Semyon and Valentina Kirlian developed a technique of high-voltage "Kirlian" photography that showed an aura of luminescence surrounding living organisms. Some researchers believe that this aura may be the same as the "electrical aura" discovered by the researchers at the University of Leningrad, and that it might represent the energy behind such paranormal phenomena as ESP and PK.

Relaxed aura
In her book *The Body Electric* (1979), Dr. Thelma Moss of the University of California School of Medicine claimed to have found a link between the electrical aura shown in Kirlian photographs and various states of mind. For example, when a subject was relaxed as a result of meditation or hypnosis, Dr. Moss discovered that Kirlian photos showed a wider and more brilliant aura.

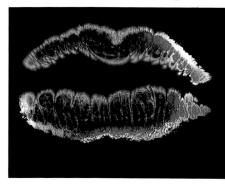

THE BRAIN AT WORK

Is the brain merely a kind of complex organic computer that operates as a self-contained unit and ceases to function with the death of our bodies? Or could it be controlled by an intangible power source — perhaps the mind — that survives beyond physical death?

A PATIENT LIES ON AN OPERATING TABLE, her scalp cut on the right side of her shaved head and a tiny segment of her skull removed to expose the surface of her brain. Yet her eyes are open; she is lucid and wide awake, nervous no doubt, but in no pain. A surgeon leans over her and gently touches an electrode to different points on the brain surface. Each point that the surgeon stimulates electrically elicits a different reaction — one causes a tingling in the patient's thumb and another makes her tongue move automatically. Although conscious, she is like a puppet, and the surgeon is pulling the strings.

"The Cutting Out of Pierre's Madness"
This painting by Flemish artist Pieter Brueghel the Elder illustrates a drastic 16th-century method of dealing with disorders of the brain. Medical practitioners of the time believed that madness originated in the head and that the only way to alleviate the condition was to cut out the offending area.

During his long career from the 1920's onward, neurosurgeon Wilder Penfield, founder of the Montreal Neurological Institute, carried out over a thousand operations like the one described above. Although there was always a medical objective, usually the treatment of epilepsy, Penfield was fascinated by the potential of this technique for studying the secrets of the brain. By observing which electrical stimulus

VITAL ORGAN
Researchers into psi are still trying to locate the precise area of the brain that might be responsible for such mysterious paranormal talents, if they exist. However, conventional medicine has made considerable progress in charting the workings of the human brain.

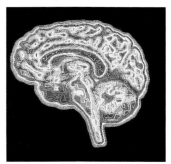

Colorful cross section
A false-color computer graphic of a cross section through the human brain.

The human brain weighs about three pounds and looks like a very big grey walnut. One of the lightest of our body organs, the brain is made up of billions of nerve cells.

Inside the brain are two cerebral hemispheres, which are linked by a bridge of about 300 million nerve fibres. Although the left and right hemispheres are very similar in structure, there are functional differences between them. The left hemisphere controls the right-hand side of the body and is generally analytical, logical, and responsible for language. The right hemisphere controls the left-hand side of the body, and is considered more emotional and intuitive.

Under control
Each hemisphere is subdivided into lobes, or regions, all of which have different functions. At the front is the frontal lobe, which deals with intellectual matters. The parietal lobes on top of the brain include sensory and motor regions, and the central temporal lobes have areas related to memory and emotion. The occipital lobe at the back of the brain governs visual input.

BEYOND ALL REASON

Some individuals who would normally be regarded as mentally retarded have turned out to have unexpected and inexplicable mental powers, such as an extraordinary facility for music, mathematical calculation, or art.

*I*N 1850 A SOUTHERN SLAVE OWNER known as Colonel Bethune came into possession of a black child known as Blind Tom. Tom had not only been born blind but was also handicapped. He was therefore unfit for plantation work, but he did have an extraordinary talent. From the earliest age he could reproduce on a piano any piece of music, however complex, that he had heard just once. He would copy and reproduce the exact rendering of the original that he had heard — and any mistakes the pianist might have made as well.

Bethune ruthlessly exploited Blind Tom's talent for financial gain, and in the process made the young slave a celebrity. Professional pianists were employed to play new pieces for Tom, so that he could expand his repertoire. Although he could neither read music nor see the keyboard, he learned to play roughly 5,000 pieces from memory, and eventually performed with success at the White House in front of President James Buchanan. Yet, controlled by Bethune, who exhibited him as a sideshow freak, Tom continued to behave like a backward child in all other areas of his life.

Blind Tom

Brilliant fools

There have been countless examples of such special talents appearing in individuals who were either of very low intelligence or even autistic. These people are called "savants." In the mid-1960's, American psychiatrist William Horowitz studied a pair of autistic identical twins, Charles and George, who had the strange ability to give the appropriate day of the week for any date, even thousands of years in the past or future. If presented with the date "September 30, 3048," they would instantly state what day of the week it was, and do so with unerring accuracy. Yet they were barely capable of speech and could not perform simple mathematical tasks.

By contrast, there have been many "calculating geniuses," people with an extraordinary talent for mental arithmetic. In 1946, a 20-year-old Belgian, Oscar Verhaeghe, was tested for his calculating ability by a committee of mathematicians. Verhaeghe could neither read nor write, and his speech was limited to the vocabulary of a small child. When asked to calculate 689 cubed, however, he produced the answer 327,082,769 in six seconds. Performing all calculations in his head, he was even able to solve $9,999,999^5$ in 40 seconds, even though the answer runs to 35 digits.

Perfect memory

Most of these special talents involve at least an element of "photographic memory," which is in itself a remarkable mental capacity. The Soviet psychologist Alexander Luria, for example, studied the case of Solomon Shereshevskii, whom he dubbed "the memory man." The psychologist would present him with a list of 50 or more unconnected numbers or words; Shereshevskii would memorize them all and repeat them without the slightest difficulty. Time made no difference to his memory.

Amazingly, even 15 years after the event he was able to repeat perfectly a list he had once learned, as well as remember every detail of the occasion on which he had learned it. Luria testified that Shereshevskii's memory was entirely visual, so that if one number in a list had been badly written — a 3 that could be mistaken for an 8, for example — he might repeat that mistake years later. As yet researchers are unable to fathom the complex and mysterious nature of the brain that allows someone with severe disabilities to be so gifted in other areas.

Amazing abilities
In the film Rain Man, *Dustin Hoffman, seen here with costar Tom Cruise, played an autistic savant with a remarkable ability to memorize numbers.*

24

produced what result, he was able to plot out a "brain map," showing the location of many human faculties — for example, where in the brain the instruction to lift the right arm would come from, and which part of the brain, when electrically stimulated, created a sense of smell.

Penfield's electrodes were even able to provoke in his patients a precise and detailed memory of a completely trivial scene experienced many years earlier, with every sight and sound relived in the mind. "A young man," Penfield wrote, "stated he was sitting at a baseball game and watching a little boy crawl under the fence to join the audience." Each time Penfield touched the same point on the brain's surface with the electrode, exactly the same past experience would unfold in all its detail. On another occasion, as the electrode stimulated her cortex, a woman on the operating table was suddenly aware of being in her kitchen and hearing the voice of her child playing outside the house. Indeed, she could hear the complete soundtrack of the past experience, including the noise of passing automobiles, which worried her because she thought the child might wander into the road and be hurt in an accident.

Mechanical feelings

If stimulation with an electric current can produce such effects, it is easy to see how some scientists have come to believe that everything human beings think and feel can be explained in electrical and chemical terms — that it is all the result of a chain of measurable physical causes and effects taking place in the brain, obeying the laws of physics and chemistry. But this, many suggest, does not explain the mystery of the human mind.

As early as the 19th century, investigators observing brain-damaged patients noted with amazement how precise the loss of mental faculty could be. Damage to one part of the brain after a stroke, for example, might make a person incapable of forming a sentence, yet leave intact the comprehension of other people's speech. Yet if a different area of the brain were put out of action, a patient might cease to understand speech, but still be able to talk fluently — in fact, might be likely to babble on endlessly and meaninglessly.

Modern research into brain damage has only served to emphasize the fact that precise abilities are situated in specific parts of the brain. In 1956, Dr. Donald Macrae and Dr. Elli Trolle from the University of California School of Medicine's Department of Neurology, observed a young man who had been the victim of a road accident. After recovering from a concussion, his vision appeared to be normal, yet he suffered from a severe disability: he could not recognize anyone, including his wife and children. Every time he saw them, he could only hope to identify them by a lengthy process of elimination and deduction. To help cope with his difficulty, his wife agreed always to wear some very striking

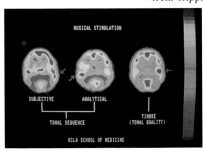

Sound effects
Different areas of the brain are capable of responding to the stimulus of sight and sound. This scan shows areas of the brain reacting to music.

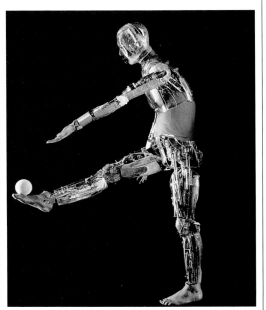

Man as machine
The philosophy of monism presents a person as little more than a complicated machine. Monists believe the mind is simply a function of the brain, and that as there is no separate "mind" or self, there cannot be any life after death.

BLINDSIGHT

In 1973 a 34-year-old Englishman, known only as D.B. for reasons of privacy, was admitted to the National Hospital, London, for brain surgery. D.B. had suffered from crippling migraine attacks since childhood, and doctors had finally decided the only solution was to remove a considerable part of his cerebral cortex.

The operation was a complete success, but as an unfortunate side effect D.B. found his sight badly impaired. Over a large area of the left side of his field of vision, he appeared to have become completely blind.

However, an ophthalmologist at the hospital, Michael D. Sanders, soon began to notice some strange anomalies in D.B.'s blindness. For example, when Sanders offered the patient his hand within the blind field, D.B. could grasp it without difficulty — even though, if asked, he denied being able to see the hand at all.

Prof. Lawrence Weiskrantz of Oxford University was alerted to the case and led a series of experiments to put D.B.'s vision to the test. When asked to guess whether an X or an O had been projected onto a screen in front of him, his "guesses" were almost 100 percent accurate.

New vision

Prof. Weiskrantz concluded that some other part of the brain had taken over from the removed cortex and was processing the unimpaired visual information still flowing in from D.B.'s undamaged eyes and optic nerve. But although his brain could still "see," and so provide correct answers to the experimenters' questions, D.B. himself was no longer conscious of seeing, and had no idea where the answers were coming from.

Scientific interest
Nobel prizewinner Roger Sperry, a scientist at the California Institute of Technology, was fascinated with the strange cases of split brains that he investigated.

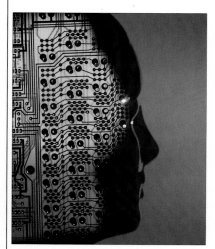

The programmable brain
The brain is often compared to a computer. Computers only work when fed programs created by a programmer, and it may be that the mind and brain interact in a similar way. Some suggest that the concept of a separate mind interacting with the body's brain leaves open the possibility that this "mind" might survive physical death.

item of clothing, such as a large hat, which he could use as an identification marker. Immediately after his accident, the patient could not even recognize his own face in a mirror. According to Macrae, "he slowly began to recognize it, but not in a flash as in the past — he relied on the hair and facial outline, and on two small moles on his left cheek." A lesion of the brain had not harmed the ability to see objects in all their detail, but had destroyed the ability to put them together in the normally simple act of recognizing a face.

One of the most remarkable scientific investigations of the brain has been the study of split-brain patients. In the 1960's scientist Roger Sperry and his colleagues at the California Institute of Technology began experiments on patients who had had the millions of nerve fibers of the *corpus callosum*, linking the left and right hemispheres of the cerebral cortex, surgically severed as a defense against epilepsy. In ordinary life the patients showed few effects of this operation — they seemed to function as usual. But under special experimental conditions, it was possible to control the information entering each half of the brain. Since the two halves were not in communication, the result apparently was to split the person into two virtually separate minds, each with its own strengths and weaknesses, and its own "personality." The left-hand side, at least in right-handed people, was skillful at speaking and writing. The right-hand side was almost mute and could understand only very simple language, but it was better at recognizing and manipulating shapes. And it was more instinctive than the analytical left brain.

Mind and mystery
It was almost impossible to communicate with the right side of the brain or to find out what it was thinking because of its limitations with language. A decade later a team of Cal Tech researchers managed to teach one patient's right brain to take control of the speaking process. The resulting

communication revealed quite different attitudes to those of the left brain in the same person. For example, when asked to say what profession it would ideally desire to follow, the left side said it wanted to be a draftsman. The right side, in contrast, expressed an overriding ambition to become a race-car driver!

Science has undoubtedly made great strides in identifying the precise locations in the brain of certain functions of the human mind — to the point that some believe they will one day be able to isolate the area of the brain that, for example, allows

> **Penfield's conclusion was that understanding brain mechanisms cannot clarify how human beings work: "None of them can explain the mind," he wrote. "The mind remains a mystery."**

individuals to understand certain words or to recognize familiar faces.

Yet a large area of irreducible mystery remains. Neurosurgeon Wilder Penfield, for example, observed that, when he made a patient lift her right arm by applying an electric charge to her brain, she felt it was something happening to her, not something she was deliberately doing. She might even try to stop the movement by holding down the arm with her left hand. It was obviously quite different to her from the experience of voluntarily raising her arm — yet if both actions were caused by the brain alone, why should there be a difference?

Change of heart
Penfield spent his whole life trying to explain things human by the activity of the brain. He identified many major brain mechanisms and mapped them in the cerebral cortex and the higher brain stem. Yet his conclusion was that understanding brain mechanisms cannot clarify how human beings work: "None of them can explain the mind," he wrote. "The mind remains a mystery."

MIND OR BRAIN?

"I do believe in the supernatural. I hope that this life will lead to some future existence where my self or soul will have another existence, with another brain, or computer if you like."
Nobel prizewinner Sir John Eccles

*I*T MAY BE OBVIOUS to us that our mental faculties — such as thinking, seeing, and feeling — are linked with the brain, but this was not always the case. In ancient Greece, for example, the philosopher Aristotle believed that the heart was the seat of reason and perception, and that the brain formed a kind of blood-cooling system.

By the 17th century, the connection between the brain and a human being's higher faculties was clearly established, but controversy continued over the exact relationship between mind and brain. French philosopher René Descartes believed that the mind was an immaterial substance that could interact with the body through the brain. The mind, he suggested, gave the order for deliberate actions — the raising of the right arm, for example — and the brain acted as a messenger, passing on the order and making sure it was carried out. The communication was two-way: the information coming in to the brain from the senses was then relayed on to the mind.

This dualism, or separateness, of mind and brain has been rejected by many scientists in the 20th century. They hold that the fantastically complex mechanism of the brain is capable of accounting for everything human beings can think, feel, and do. Our conscious awareness, they believe, is merely an epiphenomenon — an inessential side effect of the brain going about its business. In the words of philosopher Gilbert Ryle: "There is no ghost in the machine."

Materialist view

The rapid development of computers since the Second World War has reinforced this materialist view of the mind and the brain. As computers perform more and more of the activities that the human brain alone has been thought capable of — playing chess, for example — it becomes more tempting to regard the human mind as essentially a very sophisticated computer. Some computer scientists argue that, if we could construct a computer that worked exactly like the brain — an "artificial intelligence" — this machine would have as much right to be thought of as having a conscious mind as any human being.

A new reality

Are humans, then, robots, with extremely sophisticated computers on their shoulders, controlled by their brain chemistry and the electrical discharges of brain cells? There are plenty of scientists and philosophers who disagree. Some, while remaining within a strictly scientific view of the universe, have suggested that the sheer complexity of the brain creates a reality of a different kind from the rest of the material world, with its own rules. Distinguished mathematician Roger Penrose has delved into the mysteries of quantum mechanics in search of a new principle of physics that would account for the strange qualities of the mind.

Those scientists who have accepted "dualism," such as Nobel prizewinner Sir John Eccles and neurosurgeon Wilder Penfield, have had to face up to the practical problem of how an immaterial mind could interact with a physical brain. Penfield believed that the mind had to have some form of energy at its disposal, with which it could influence brain cells. Researchers speculated that if the mind had such an energy, it was clearly possible that it might be able to survive separately from the body, and even to communicate directly with other minds, as in telepathy, or to affect certain physical objects, as in psychokinesis.

Mind and body
René Descartes was a dualist; his view was that the mind and body are separate but can affect each other, so that what happens in the body can produce effects on the mind, and vice versa.

Paranormal possibilities

Not all believers in ESP and other paranormal phenomena believe in the immaterial mind. Some think that the paranormal can be explained by the special and unique powers of the brain, entirely physical but as yet undetected by science. But if there is a "ghost in the machine," it might make paranormal happenings more likely and more credible.

MASS HYSTERIA

We describe people as "hysterical" when they appear to have lost conscious control over their behavior. Screaming and uncontrollable laughter or crying are the usual signs of the condition. But what causes the spread of such hysterical behavior from one person to another?

THE WORD HYSTERIA is derived from the Greek for uterus, and hysteria was once thought to be a weakness of the mind occurring only in women, caused by a diseased womb and resulting in loss of control of the body. By the 19th century, however, doctors had realized that the condition had a psychological origin, and the term was being used to describe a wide variety of states, including hallucinations and trances.

Many traditional cultures have encouraged hysterical behavior. The shaman, or medicine man, was usually chosen for his role because he was capable of going into trances in which he was supposedly able to commune with the spirits. Tribal societies often induced hysteria to help with healing. Sick people were put into trances, in which they had convulsions and drifted into comas, with the intention that the spirits would help them to recover from their sickness while they were in this receptive state. Fierce drumming and dancing contributed to the hysterical atmosphere.

Tortured image
A line drawing of one of 19th-century French hypnotist and neurologist Jean-Martin Charcot's hysterical patients. Charcot was intrigued by the strange power the mind has over the body.

Loss of control

Mass hysteria occurs when a large number of people assembled together in one place appear to lose their self-control. This type of behavior happens most commonly nowadays at rock concerts, but it has been known to take place at political and religious rallies.

But what precisely sparks the spread of such behavior? Could some form of psychic communication between human minds be responsible for the spread of such outlandish loss of control? This explanation certainly seems more plausible when considering that the term *mass hysteria* also describes the spread of psychologically produced symptoms of illness from person to person. Sometimes whole groups of people are struck down with what seems to be a specific sickness, only to recover quite quickly. The first person to have the symptoms sets a pattern, and then others follow, as if in imitation. This

The word *hysteria* is derived from the Greek for uterus, and hysteria was once thought to be a weakness of the mind occurring only in women, caused by a diseased womb and resulting in loss of control of the body.

Beatlemania
Rock music fans are often swept up into displays of mass hysteria. The Beatlemania of the 1960's resulted in astonishing scenes of distraught, weeping, and fainting fans, which took place at airports and concert stages worldwide.

Fatal devotion
In 1978, over 900 members of a California religious sect called the People's Temple committed mass suicide in the jungles of Guyana, on the northern coast of South America. The followers drank potassium cyanide mixed with a fizzy drink on the orders of their psychopathic leader Rev. Jim Jones. No one knows exactly how so many people could be persuaded to kill themselves, but the collective suicide may have been an example of mass hysteria, the will of the group overpowering that of the individual.

phenomenon usually happens in a school or similar institution, and a single charismatic personality often triggers the effect. However, in the September 1981 edition of the *Journal of Occupational Medicine*, Dr. Michael J. Colligan tackled the issue of hysterical outbreaks in American factories and concluded that the working environment, new working practices,

---

Many animals have a method of communication that we do not yet fully understand. Perhaps mass hysteria is a relic of some similar human capacity to communicate.

---

and stress are the most likely triggers for mass hysteria, and that "the experienced symptoms are by no means imaginary or illusory."

Yet this type of hysterical contagion might have an evolutionary explanation. Many animals have a method of communication that we do not yet fully understand, such as the ability of birds to stay together in flocks while traveling huge distances. Perhaps mass hysteria is a relic of some similar human capacity to communicate.

Another possible explanation for this strange unspoken link between humans is the existence of scent molecules called pheromones. Researchers have discovered that pheromones play a part in sexual attraction, but believe that these molecules may also influence our behavior in other ways. Women living in close contact with each other often have their menstrual periods at the same time, and pheromones might be responsible for this effect. Despite the existence of these molecules, certain paranormal researchers prefer to emphasize the possibility that some form of collective mind forms the basis for such instances of unspoken communication.

Hitler and the Reichstag
Dictator Adolf Hitler seemed to understand how to manipulate mass behavior. He was able to incite hysterical outbursts from many of his followers.

PAINLESS SEIZURES
In the early 18th century the cemetery of St. Médard in Paris became renowned for a number of miraculous cures that were said to have taken place at the tomb of a little-known deacon, François de Pâris.

Waiting for a miracle
This engraving shows hopeful pilgrims surrounding François de Pâris's tomb at St. Médard.

Convulsionaries
But in early 1731 eager visitors to the cemetery became the victims of a strange epidemic when they were seized by convulsions, which passed from person to person, apparently as a result of contagious hysteria. Victims of the epidemic became known as convulsionaries, and appeared to be completely impervious to pain while in this hysterical state.

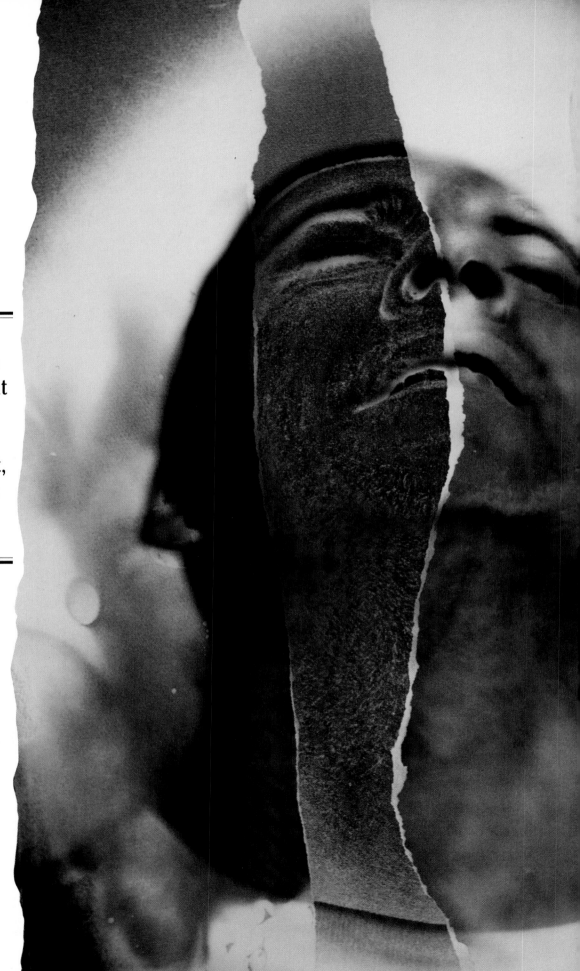

"I could see
and hear in a
totally different
way. I had
gained my
enlightenment,
the shaman's
light of brain
and body...."

LOST POWERS

In modern Western societies, most people consider those claiming to have psychic powers as oddities. But in ancient times, the early equivalents of today's mediums, channelers, or diviners were not viewed as freaks on the fringes of society. They were important public figures. This remains true today in those parts of the world where tribal societies have survived relatively intact.

FROM THE TUNGUS AND INUITS of the Arctic to the Jivaro of the Amazon basin, tribal peoples have traditionally depended on their shamans, or medicine men, to cure them of illness and to supply many other vital services, both practical and spiritual — from controlling weather conditions to communing with the spirit world.

The shaman, usually a male, may be chosen by heredity, succeeding his father in the role, or he may be marked at an early age by his unusual behavior — having visions of spirits or gods, developing a taste for solitude, and wandering off alone into the forests or mountains for weeks on end, or becoming chronically absentminded and talking or singing to himself all day.

Chosen by the gods

But whether born to be a shaman or, as shamanic belief would have it, chosen by the spirits or gods, the would-be shaman generally must go through a dramatic crisis of initiation before he can adopt the role. In some cases, he may begin to see visions, working up to a climax in which he has convulsive fits and falls into a long period of unconsciousness. While the initiate is in this deathlike state, apparently induced by the power of suggestion, he experiences a horrific dream or vision. This ordeal prepares him for habitual contact with the spirit world. In some cases, he may witness his own death at the hands of devils. One shamanic initiate recorded that, in his vision, devils sliced off his head and then put it to one side so that he could watch while they dismembered the remainder of his body.

Changed perception

When the chosen young man recovers consciousness following his visionary ordeal, he will have the exceptional spiritual powers necessary to act as a shaman. In the 1930's one Inuit shaman told the Danish Arctic explorer Knud Rasmussen what it was like to have attained that magical status: "I could see and hear in a totally different way. I had gained my enlightenment, the shaman's light of brain and body...."

ACCEPTING ESP
Dr. Margaret Mead, who was one of America's foremost anthropologists, pointed out that ESP is not considered unusual in some cultures. She suggested that psychic ability may be more common among people who recognize and support its development and use. Mead encouraged the acceptance of parapsychology as a legitimate area of study: "The whole history of scientific advance is full of scientists investigating phenomena that the establishment did not believe were there." In 1969 Mead persuaded the American Association for the Advancement of Science to admit the Parapsychological Association as an affiliate.

31

All the shaman's powers apparently depend on his ability to enter a state of trance in which, according to shamanic beliefs, his soul is separated from his body. This trance may be induced in a variety of ways. In some societies, the shaman fasts and mortifies his flesh in a hermit-like solitude until the necessary visions appear or spirit voices speak. More often, there is a public ritual with insistent drumming and rhythmic dancing. The suggestive power of the music and dance is sufficient to put the shaman into a trance state. In South America particularly, the shaman and other tribesmen may consume various hallucinogenic plants or drinks.

When in a trance, some shamans experience possession and speak with the voices of spirits — a practice very similar to that of spiritualist mediums. But most shamans simply provide a running commentary on what they witness and undergo during their psychic voyage.

A Kalahari bushman

BUSH TELEGRAPH
In his book *Lost World of the Kalahari* (1958) explorer Laurens van der Post described an enlightening experience he had while hunting for eland with a group of Kalahari bushmen in South Africa. About 50 miles from the home camp, the bushmen cornered and killed an animal. One of the hunters told Post that the women in their encampment would know of the killing almost immediately. When Post looked puzzled, the hunter tapped his chest and explained, "We bushpeople have a wire here that brings us news."

Superhuman shaman

Shamans believe that, during a trance, their souls are separated from their bodies. This permits them to fly through the air at will, both across earthly distances and through the supernatural spaces of heaven and hell. They can capture souls and steal or return them to their owners. They may communicate with spirits and with the souls of the dead. They may be capable of becoming invisible or of disguising themselves as animals — usually the jaguar in South America. They can perceive events far off in time and space, and can kill an enemy from a distance. And they are impervious to both fire and pain.

There is no question that shamans do experience visions and the illusion of flight. In 1961 anthropologist Michael J. Harner, who was initiated into the shamanic practices of the Jivaro Indian tribe in the upper Amazon basin, reported his own dramatic experience during a trance in much the same terms as the Indians themselves:

"I found myself, although awake, in a world literally beyond my wildest dreams. I met bird-headed people, as

> **"I found myself...in a world literally beyond my wildest dreams. I met bird-headed people, as well as dragonlike creatures who explained that they were the true gods of this world."**

well as dragonlike creatures who explained that they were the true gods of this world. I enlisted the services of other spirit helpers in attempting to fly through the far reaches of the galaxy."

But the psychic flight does not always entail a vision of the spirit world. It may include a journey to another part of our own planet. Among the Jivaro Indians, shamans are frequently asked to see what a person is doing at some distant location — to check, for example, whether a woman is being faithful in the absence of her partner. Or the shaman may be asked to summon up the vision of a crime that has been committed, in order to identify the perpetrators as effectively as a video camera monitoring the scene. Of course, it is extremely difficult to substantiate such claims, but in 1946 anthropologist

Spirit mask
This shaman's spirit mask is from the northwest coast of the United States and dates from the mid-19th century.

Tomas Roessner produced intriguing evidence for the validity of shamanic visions. His claims were based on his experiences living among Indian tribesmen in the remote Ucayali River region of eastern Peru. The Indians, who had no contact with modern civilization, claimed to be in the habit of making spirit voyages to view distant cities. According to Roessner, "Indians have asked white men what those strange things are that run so swiftly along the street: they had seen automobiles which, of course, they were not acquainted with."

Tribal responsibilities

The perceived practical value of the shaman to his tribe is manifold. He is responsible for controlling the weather, identifying the location of game, and interceding with the spirits to guarantee good hunting. He foretells the future and locates valuable objects that have been lost. His central function, however, is to cure the sick. In the shamanic view of the world, illness is the result either of an evil object entering the body or of the soul of the patient being stolen. The shaman can embark on a psychic voyage to find the stolen soul and return it to its rightful owner, or he can suck the evil object out of the sick person's body.

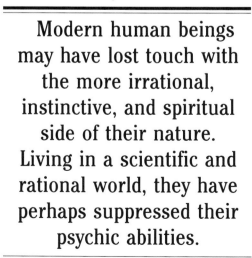

Jivaro shaman

Paranormal powers

Some of the powers claimed by shamans are familiar to modern students of the paranormal. The experience of flight out of the body and of "seeing" places at a distance is generally equivalent to out-of-body experiences and clairvoyance. The shaman's healing practices are in many ways akin to those of Western faith healers, and the trance state of a shaman is so similar to that of some spiritualist mediums that anthropologists habitually refer to the trance-inducing tribal gatherings as "séances." There is a far higher proportion of shamans in tribal society than psychics in modern industrial societies. Among the Jivaro tribe, to take an extreme example, one in four males is a shaman. One possible explanation of this is that modern human beings may have lost touch with the more irrational, instinctive, and spiritual side of their nature. Living in a scientific and rational world, they have perhaps suppressed their psychic abilities. Just as the human sense of smell has declined in importance because people depend instead on their sense of sight, so psychic powers, if they exist, may have atrophied through lack of use, ignored by the rational self. If this view is correct, then prehistoric man, living well before the age of science and reason, may well have been more in touch with the powers of the mind than we are today.

In the 1950's an Australian psychic researcher, Ronald Rose, set out to test this hypothesis by subjecting aborigines to rigorous ESP and PK experiments of the kind pioneered by Dr. J. B. Rhine at Duke University. Rose described the subjects of his tests as

> Modern human beings may have lost touch with the more irrational, instinctive, and spiritual side of their nature. Living in a scientific and rational world, they have perhaps suppressed their psychic abilities.

semicivilized — in other words, they had abandoned their traditional way of life and largely adopted white Australian customs. But Rose felt that they were still

David Leslie

ELEPHANT HUNT

Stories about the amazing psychic powers of African witch doctors have been told for over a century. David Leslie, an English hunter and merchant, reported a typical tale in 1875.

Leslie's elephant hunters had been sent out with orders to meet him at a specific place on a particular day. When the hunters did not appear, Leslie went to visit the local witch doctor to see if he could tell him what had happened to the men. The witch doctor asked how many hunters were missing and what their names were. He then lit eight fires, one for each missing hunter, threw some roots on the fire, drank an unspecified medicine, and went into a trance.

Reading the ashes

After about 10 minutes he came out of the trance and raked through the ashes of each fire. He then informed Leslie what had happened to the hunters: One had died of fever and his gun was lost; another was killed by an elephant but his gun had been recovered; a third had killed four elephants and was bringing back the tusks. According to the witch doctor, the surviving hunters would be back in about three months, traveling by a different route than the one that had originally been agreed upon.

According to Leslie's report, the surviving hunters did in fact return three months later, and confirmed the witch doctor's prediction.

close enough, in evolutionary terms, to their primitive ancestors to make the experiment worthwhile. The PK experiments turned out to be a total failure, with worse results than those usually obtained by the American college students often used by psychic researchers. But in the ESP experiments, performed with cards, 7 out of 12 aborigines recorded scores significantly better than chance.

If in prehistoric times human beings were more in touch with their psychic powers than today, it is not surprising that a strong faith in such powers persisted in the early civilizations of Greece and Rome. In ancient Greece belief in the divinatory abilities of oracles was almost universal, shared by the common people and kings and potentates alike. Delphi was the site of the most famous oracle, that of Apollo.

Ritual behavior
Spear-carrying aborigines daubed with ash and mud perform an ancient tribal ritual. Such rituals were reportedly used to help hunters to "see" the location of their prey, before they set out in the vital search for food.

Prophetic trance
The Delphic oracle's prophecies were expressed through a priestess known as the Pythia, or pythoness, an uneducated woman who uttered the prophecies while in a trance. Her state of trance was probably induced by a series of ritual actions — sitting in the seat of the god Apollo, nibbling a laurel leaf, surrounded by the smoke of powerful incense. Like a medium communicating with a spirit-being in a séance, the Pythia took on a completely different voice when prophesying, as the god spoke through her. Although evidence from so ancient a time is hard to examine and assess, it seems clear that the priestesses who related the predictions of the oracles were what we would call "mediums" or "psychics." The often unintelligible utterances of

The temple of Jupiter at Baalbek, in the Lebanon

the Pythia at Delphi were translated into verse by the priests of the oracle. The kings and emperors who sent to ask the oracle for information about the future often received a totally ambiguous answer, which they had to interpret as best they could. The practical uselessness of so many of the oracle's prophecies tends, of course, to encourage a skeptical view of the whole business. But much of what we know of the oracle at Delphi and other oracles is

> # Her state of trance was probably induced by a series of ritual actions — sitting in the seat of the god Apollo, nibbling a laurel leaf, surrounded by the smoke of incense.

not inconsistent with what some researchers believe about psi. There were occasions, for example, when the oracle answered a question before it was put, suggesting perhaps a telepathic reading of the inquirer's mind.

Many famous stories are reported from ancient times, especially of rulers attempting to test the psychic powers of the oracles. In about A.D. 100, the Roman emperor Trajan is said to have set a test for the oracle of Jupiter at Baalbek in Syria (now in the Lebanon). This oracle was famous for its ability to read messages in a sealed container. To trick the oracle, Trajan sent to Baalbek blank tablets of stone in a sealed box, asking for an answer to the questions written on them. The oracle sent back the box, with the seal unbroken, and an answer — a blank sheet of papyrus.

THE PSI SOCIETY

The psychic powers that may be displayed by certain exceptional people today may be all that is left of a natural ability once used extensively by humankind. This, at least, is the belief of those who are convinced that the origins of our present civilization are to be found on the lost continent of Atlantis.

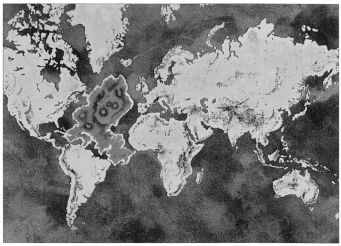

Lost civilization?
According to accounts supplied by 19th-century Theosophists, the continent of Atlantis was formerly located in the Atlantic.

IT WAS PLATO, THE GREEK PHILOSOPHER and master storyteller, who introduced the world to Atlantis in about 355 B.C. in two of his famous dialogues, the *Timaeus* and the *Critias*. Claiming the story came from ancient Egyptian records (none of which has ever been found) Plato told of a great empire that existed 9,000 years earlier on an island or continent. Its armies struck out at its neighbors, but "afterward there occurred violent earthquakes and floods; and in a single day and night of destruction all your warlike men in a body sank into the earth, and the island of Atlantis in like manner disappeared in the depths of the sea."

Loss of virtue

Plato's dialogues contain such detailed accounts of the engineering and architectural feats of the Atlanteans that some scholars are certain they are based on fact rather than fable. The dialogues describe superb buildings; temples decorated with ivory, gold and silver; huge statues; and sophisticated systems of waterways and baths. But, according to Plato, when the people of Atlantis began to lose their love of wisdom and virtue and started to become greedy, corrupt, and domineering, Zeus, god of gods, decided to punish them and collected all the gods together "and spoke as follows...."

And there, tantalizingly, Plato's story ends. He never completed his trilogy. But others have attempted to build on his story ever since, and none more so than certain occultists claiming to have gained special insight into the history of Atlantis through their paranormal powers.

In the 1880's Madame Helena Blavatsky, the somewhat suspect founder of the Theosophical Society, challenged Darwin's theory of evolution by suggesting that several races once lived on earth, among them the Atlanteans. English occultist Walter Scott-Elliot worked with Madame Blavatsky on developing her unorthodox theories and he claimed to

The Greek island of Santorini

have used clairvoyant vision to discover that Atlantis was occupied by various tribes, including aboriginals who stood 10 to 12 feet tall. Scott-Elliot's complex account of racial evolution over many thousands of years includes the claim that among the inventions of Atlantean scientists were aircraft that could take off vertically and were directed by mind power. In order to expand on the Theosophists' discoveries regarding Atlantis, Rudolph Steiner, founder of the Anthroposophical Society, is purported to have consulted the Akashic Records, a register of everything that has ever happened to humankind. (The precise location of these records remains a mystery.) Steiner believed that the Atlanteans used a "life force" to power their aircraft and healed the sick through the use of magic words.

Is all this just wild speculation? Not for the various people who believed they were Atlanteans in previous lives, because of personal readings they received in the early 1940's from the famous trance clairvoyant and healer Edgar Cayce. In his descriptions of those lives Cayce spoke of inventions that were in use in Atlantis, one of which was very similar to today's laser beam.

The most likely geographical position of Atlantis is in the Aegean, since archeological evidence suggests that the myth was inspired by the Greek island of Thera (now known as Santorini), which was devastated, but not completely destroyed, by a huge volcanic eruption in 1500 B.C. Its people had close ties with Minoan Crete, and there are remarkable cultural similarities between Crete at that time and Plato's descriptions of Atlantis. Thus Plato's account may have had some basis in fact.

Multitalented
This 19th-century poster advertises the amazing powers of Toby the pig.

ANIMAL POWER

We know that animals have many physical abilities that humans cannot match. But do all their special talents have a rational explanation or might animals be displaying paranormal powers?

NIMALS HAVE MANY ABILITIES that humans lack. No person can run as fast as a cheetah or walk upside down on a ceiling like a spider. The eyes of a shark are 10 times more sensitive to light than our own. The built-in radar of the bat and the long life-span of the giant tortoise are additional examples of animal capacities that people cannot equal.

The impressive and, in some cases, unexplained powers of animals have been recognized for thousands of years. Many ancient peoples, including the Egyptians, worshipped certain animals as gods, and in other cultures gods have been described as part human and part animal. Ancient Abyssinia (now Ethiopia) was supposedly ruled at one time by a dog-king, who wore a gown and a gold crown. Priests interpreted the creature's barks and the taps of his paws as edicts.

Working in unison
Social insects such as ants have a telecommunications system which researchers have been unable to fathom. The colony acts in harmony, almost like a single organism. Some researchers into anpsi believe the ants may make use of some form of telepathy.

Psychic possibilities

In fairness, animals may be as likely to possess unexplained powers as humans. Many stories describe the uncanny ability of various creatures to predict natural disasters and man-made accidents. Animals also display an amazing rapport with people — and reportedly with ghostly phenomena as well. Some creatures, it is said, will not enter the same buildings that humans believe are haunted.

The study of ESP in animals is called anpsi, short for *ani*mal *psi*. Research into anpsi began in the early 1920's when Dr. W. Bechterev published a report describing experiments on influencing the behavior of a dog telepathically. Objects were placed around the room and experimenters concentrated on the object they wanted the subject, a fox terrier called Pikki, to bring back to them. According to Dr. Bechterev, the dog usually chose the selected object.

Navigation skills
The arctic tern flies 12,000 miles a year, from winter feeding grounds in South America to summer breeding grounds on the Arctic tundra. Many animals navigate enormous distances in ways that remain a mystery to researchers.

Animal misnomer
In 1986 a month-old kitten called Gribouille, meaning "short-sighted fool," was given away by its French owner and was taken to Raventlinger in Germany. But after spending only four days there, the kitten disappeared. Two years later, on July 24th, the story goes, the cat turned up at the home of its original owner in Tannency, France, having traveled a distance of over 600 miles.

Short-sighted expectations
Gribouille back with its original French owner.

In 1950, researchers at Duke University's parapsychology laboratory began studying unexplained animal behavior that might reflect anpsi. Dr. Rhine studied the possible ESP abilities of rats, cats, and pigeons. He even ran tests for the army, which wanted to know if German Shepherd Dogs could be trained to find land mines using ESP. The dogs performed well, but Dr. Rhine suggested the animals may have been using a sharp sense of smell rather than psychic power. Staff members also collected stories of unusual experiences from different parts of the world, involving a range of species. Investigators suggested several kinds of behavior that could involve anpsi:

◆ **Psi trailing:** An animal separated from a person to whom it is attached follows the person to an unfamiliar area.

◆ **Death reactions:** Animals may react to the approaching death of a master, or may have premonitions of their own death.

◆ **Reactions to impending danger:** Danger to people or to the animal itself from a natural disaster may prompt unusual behavior, perhaps in an attempt to raise the alarm.

◆ **Homing:** Many species show an instinct that guides them back toward their original home.

◆ **Cases of possible telepathy:** In a range of situations, animals sometimes show that they are responding to an owner's unspoken wishes.

Disaster alert

A variety of animals show remarkable sensitivity to impending earthquakes. A 1976 conference at the Center for Earthquake Research at Menlo Park in California discussed the substantial evidence that suggests that creatures are aware of impending disaster long before humans are alerted. For example, deer jump up and down, fish leap out of the water, and

> **Dogs seem especially sensitive to approaching catastrophe, and their insistent howling and barking has been noted before a number of earthquakes.**

chickens suddenly fly into trees when faced with such a situation. Dogs seem especially sensitive to approaching catastrophe, and their insistent howling and barking has been noted before a number of earthquakes. Animals of all kinds have been noticed fleeing areas hurriedly before earthquakes or other natural disasters occur.

The Rocky Mountains, Colorado

Long-distance travel

In the fall monarch butterflies migrate southward from Hudson Bay to Florida, Texas, and California, where they hibernate after traveling nearly 2,000 miles. The longest distance recorded for the flight of a monarch is 1,870 miles, but researchers are not clear as to how the monarchs navigate such huge distances and in such large numbers.

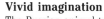

Monarch butterfly

Rockies in winter

The homing abilities of dogs may be due to a superior sense of direction, or even some unknown sixth sense. In 1923 a family from Silverton, Oregon, lost their collie, Bobbie, while on vacation in Walcott, Indiana. Six months later Bobbie reportedly arrived back at Silverton, having traveled over 2,000 miles. During Bobbie's long journey home through Illinois, Iowa, Nebraska, Colorado, Wyoming, and Idaho, he had even made his way across the Rocky Mountains in winter.

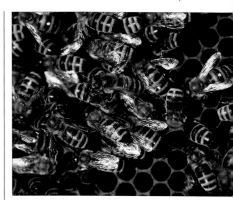

Hive of activity

Bees appear to be aware of impending changes in the weather. When a thunderstorm is about to strike, the insects become very agitated and return to the hive in large numbers.

Vivid imagination

The Russian animal trainer and clown Vladimir Durov believed that he had devised a way of giving orders to dogs by telepathic means. He did so simply by vividly imagining what he wanted the dog to do. Durov claimed that his dogs performed exactly what he wanted at precisely the time he was instructing them telepathically.

Bad habits

Animal trainer Vladimir Durov with one of his first pupils, Bishka.

CHAPTER TWO

MIND OVER MIND

The word **hypnos** *is Greek for "sleep," but the hypnotic state is far removed from sleeping. In fact, studies of hypnosis provide the nearest thing we have to a window on the operations of the unconscious mind.*

Hypnosis produces an altered state of consciousness. Under the supervision of an expert hypnotist nearly everyone can be hypnotized lightly and some people are deeply affected. And hypnosis may even improve some faculties, such as memory.

The use of hypnotic techniques goes back to at least the time of the ancient Greeks and Egyptians. Both cultures had special hypnotic centers where people went to receive help with their problems. Hypnotic methods similar to those in use today were used to discover the nature of a patient's dreams, which priests then

HYPNOTIC TECHNIQUES

A number of methods are used to hypnotize people. Subjects are generally told to listen to the hypnotist, concentrating on what is being suggested. Hypnotists often ask people to focus on an object above eye level, so that optical muscles become tired.

Complete relaxation

The concentration method may be combined with progressive relaxation. The subject eases every muscle as the hypnotist speaks repeatedly of "waves of relaxation" washing over the body. The person is encouraged to feel drowsy so that his or her eyes close involuntarily. Another technique for relaxation is to have

A hypnotist at work

a subject clench one fist, letting all bodily tension flow into the hand. Unclenching the fist supposedly lets the built-up tension escape.

Some subjects may be told to count backward in ones or threes, while concentrating on what the hypnotist is saying.

Return journey

Hypnotic trances can be ended by reversing procedures. Subjects may be instructed to imagine themselves going up on an escalator or in an elevator. Generally, an even simpler method is used. The hypnotist may count backward from 10 to 1 or simply instruct the subject to wake up.

studied for clues about what anxieties were worrying the dreamer.

These ancient civilizations also had sleep temples for the sick, where music, drugs, and repetitive speech were used to induce sleep. While asleep, sufferers were told that their symptoms would disappear, thus helping to effect a cure.

Centuries later, a Swiss physician, Paracelsus (1493–1541), put forward the idea that the stars influenced humans through some kind of magnetic force. Another doctor, Van Helmont (1577–1644), developed this idea by suggesting that each person radiated a kind of strong "animal magnetism," which had an influence on others. These speculations were the background for the growth of hypnosis that took place during the latter half of the 18th century.

Franz Anton Mesmer (1734–1815) was a graduate of the University of Vienna Medical Faculty. His doctoral thesis discussed the possibility of the stars and planets influencing our powers to cure. Mesmer began practicing as a physician in 1767 and for six years he worked as a conventional doctor. But in 1773, a young, female relative, Franzl Oesterlin, came to visit him. And her stay was to have profound repercussions.

Depressing symptoms

Oesterlin suffered from a severe illness that included such symptoms as convulsions, depression, temporary blindness, and hysterical spasms. Mesmer tried to treat her with conventional medicine, but nothing seemed to help.

Finally, a university colleague suggested Mesmer try fixing metallic plates to the patient to restore her magnetic "harmony." When the girl's condition improved following this treatment, Mesmer was reminded of his doctoral thesis. In it he had theorized that the two halves of the human body

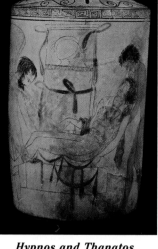

Hypnos and Thanatos
The gods of sleep and death transport a dead man to the "otherworld."

acted like the poles of a magnet, and that illness was caused by an improper distribution of this magnetism. When Mesmer discovered that he could improve his patients' conditions simply by passing his hands over their bodies and downwards towards their feet, using no metallic plates, he decided that his own body must be a magnetic channel.

The marquis de Puységur (1751–1825) became one of Mesmer's followers. Puységur's contribution to the history of hypnosis was to describe a state like a modern hypnotic trance in which patients can walk, speak, and follow instructions, which he called "artificial somnambulism." Puységur discovered this trance state by accident when he applied Mesmer's methods to a young shepherd, Victor, who suffered from

Uncharacteristic behavior
Puységur watched as his hypnotic subject Victor lapped milk from a saucer like a cat.

hysterical convulsions. Using Mesmer's techniques, which became known as mesmerism, Puységur put the shepherd into a quiet, sleeping stupor. Victor then did whatever Puységur told him to, even when asked to behave like a cat.

Puységur developed this technique further by asking his patients to describe their symptoms and problems while in a trance, an approach that is still practiced in modern hypnotic treatment. Puységur believed that the mesmerist controlled the patient by the power of his will and that the mesmerist's brain secreted fluid with the power to cure. This fluid passed along nerves and then to the patient.

James Braid (1795–1860) was a Scottish surgeon who became interested in mesmerism, but he rejected the idea of a magnetic fluid. At first, Braid was convinced that the trance state was related closely to natural sleep. Braid mistakenly thought that protracted eye fixation brought about a state of fatigue in part of the brain. He believed a subject entered a condition of nervous sleep that he termed "neurohypnotism," later shortened to "hypnotism." But he was correct in a sense, in that he realized there was no direct physiological link between a hypnotist and his or her subject.

Revival of interest

After Braid's death, hypnotism fell out of favor with much of the medical profession until the 1880's, when a French neurologist, Jean-Martin Charcot (1825–1893), revived interest by his insistence that hysterical symptoms such as paralysis, deafness, and blindness could be influenced by hypnosis. While Charcot's ideas have turned out to be largely erroneous, his endorsement did encourage others to try hypnotic techniques.

Another French doctor, A. A. Liébeault (1823–1903), pioneered the use of hypnosis in general practice. Liébeault thought everyone was susceptible to hypnosis, and he placed great emphasis on rapport between doctor and patient. He made a point of stressing the fact that he possessed no mysterious power.

Jean-Martin Charcot

Modern experimental studies of hypnosis began with the work of Clark L. Hull at Yale University in the early 1930's. Hull and his co-workers showed that it is possible to influence human behavior by hypnotic suggestion. For example, they demonstrated changes in responses to sensory stimuli and also indicated that childhood memories become more accessible.

Experiments with hypnosis expanded greatly in the 1950's and 1960's and standardized scales of suggestibility were devised by E. R. Hilgard of Stanford University in 1961. One of Hilgard's most interesting findings was that children between 8 and 12 are easiest to hypnotize. (Young children find concentration difficult and older children become less suggestible.)

In the first half of the 20th century, most medical personnel continued to regard hypnosis very warily. But by 1958 the American Medical Association had acknowledged that hypnosis could be useful medically. However, many people remain suspicious about what can happen when hypnosis is used.

Fixed stare
Braid's hypnotic technique had patients staring at an object near to, and slightly above, their eyes.

THE STATE OF TRANCE
Once the explanation of "animal magnetism" was generally rejected, a new definition of the trance state of consciousness was needed. In 1843 the British physician James Braid used the words *hypnotic trance* to describe a peculiar condition of the nervous system. Braid believed the trance was a form of "nervous sleep," or partial suppression of the brain's function.

Contact with the mind
Later definitions have added little to Braid's theory. In 1969 another British physician, Stephen Black, described the trance as a "sleepless state of decreased or altered consciousness." This was induced by "constrictive or

Animal magnetism
An 18th-century hypnotist projects magnetism from the palms of his hands.

rhythmic stimuli." It was different from ordinary sleep because of the presence of "relative awareness or increased suggestibility." The trance was a state in which direct contact could be made with the unconscious mind.

Measuring the trance
The hypnotic trance has been very elusive in laboratory examinations. American research psychologists Leslie LeCron and Jean Bordeaux deny that there is a single hypnotic state. They have drawn up a scoring system for indicating the depth of hypnosis, ranging from 1 (physical relaxation) to 50 (a stuporous condition in which all spontaneous activity is inhibited).

A MAGNETIC THEORY

The use of magnets to treat disease goes back to ancient times. In the 18th century Mesmer's controversial salon followed physician Paracelsus's 16th-century ideas about the magnetic properties of the body.

High drama
Mesmer's salon, with its baquet, or tub, was a fashionable spot, where people came to touch iron rods and be touched by mesmerists. Places had to be booked in advance, like seats at the opera. Mirrors on the wall together with closed curtains contributed to the theatrical atmosphere of the salon. On the right of this picture can be seen a back room with a small, separate, free, but little used, tub for the poor. When the salon was shut down, a satisfied customer protested in vain: "If I owe the health I enjoy to an illusion, permit me to make use of an agent that does not exist and yet heals me."

FRANZ ANTON MESMER believed sickness was caused by a stoppage to the vital yet undefined fluid that he believed to be constantly flowing through the body. He suggested that individuals could control the fluid's action by massaging the body's magnetic "poles," thus overcoming obstacles to the flow. This massage then induced convulsions and a "crisis" that restored a person's health.

Mesmer and his followers sometimes treated individuals by sitting with the patient's knees between their own. The therapist ran his fingers over the patient's body, seeking the poles of the small magnets that made up the great magnet of the body as a whole.

Mesmer's many patients, who were mainly women, regarded him with awe, but for Mesmer the technique was rooted in science. He believed that disease and healing were part of natural cosmic law, and that space was

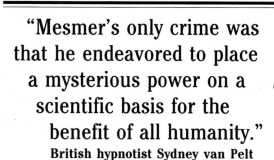

Franz Anton Mesmer

An 18th-century magnetic tub

> ## "Mesmer's only crime was that he endeavored to place a mysterious power on a scientific basis for the benefit of all humanity."
> **British hypnotist Sydney van Pelt**

filled with special "animal magnetism" through which "the magnetic influence of the heavens affects all parts of the body." Any interruption in the natural ebb and flow of this universal and invisible substance had a direct effect on the nerves, thus causing disease. The healer's function was to restore balance by acting as a human magnet and channeling the vital force to the affected area.

Mesmer's group therapy relied on a combination of magnetic theory and atmospheric suggestion. Background music played as the patients sat around large oak tubs filled with water, stones, and iron filings. Metal rods protruded from holes in the top of the tubs, and sufferers held these rods against ailing parts of their bodies. This therapeutic approach was used to treat a variety of problems, from paralysis and ear trouble to insomnia, and liver disorders.

Mesmer would enter the room grandly, wearing a silk lilac robe and touching patients with a long, iron wand. He passed his hands over clients

Skeptical commissioner
Benjamin Franklin was a member of the commission that rejected any scientific "magnetic" basis for Mesmer's techniques.

and fixed his eyes upon them. He prompted the group to talk about their feelings and actively encouraged highly emotional responses that often led to hysteria and even unconsciousness.

In 1784 King Louis XVI of France set up a royal commission to investigate Mesmer. The team included a number of well-known scientists, including Benjamin Franklin, who was American ambassador to France at the time.

The commission concluded that it was imagination rather than magnetism that was effecting any cures. According to the commission, any improvement in a patient's health was due to Mesmer's

> ## "I am accused of being a common cheat, and those who believe in me are taunted as being fools. Such is apt to be the fate of new truths."
> **Anton Mesmer**

verbal suggestions that he or she would become better. Mesmer's licence to practice was removed as a result of the commission's negative report.

Magnetic touch

The report also suggested that Mesmer's techniques were of a dubious moral nature. There undoubtedly was something erotic about the technique, which often resulted in ladies crying out ecstatically during the "magetic" touching sessions.

Mesmer died in relative obscurity, but "mesmerism," the therapy to which he gave his name, continued to develop and change. In the light of present knowledge, it seems that he did employ certain recognizable techniques. Mesmer certainly made good use of what psychiatrists now call "abreaction" or release of tension by the reliving of a traumatic experience.

Inga Gaiduchenkova
In the late 1980's a young girl in Byelorussia astonished experts by her ability to magnetize almost everything except glass. Patients with circulation difficulties benefited from the warmth of her arms and hands. Could this effect be similar to the kind of magnetic power that Mesmer believed he possessed?

Puységur's tree
According to the theory of magnetism, if a tree were magnetized, a person who touched it would have a "crisis" or convulsions. The marquis de Puységur apparently magnetized an elm tree, and contact with the tree via ropes put patients into a deep sleep.

Feeling no pain
Hypnotized subjects who have been told they will not be burned can touch a candle flame and feel no pain. If told there will be no blister, no blister appears. Conversely, if told they will be touched by something red hot, subjects will cry out in pain and a blister will form even if the object is cold.

HYPNOTIC TREATMENT

Hypnotism has been regarded with varying degrees of skepticism over the centuries. Today it is taught to only a minority of medical and psychology students. However, interest has been growing in recent years as a result of the publicity given to success stories.

IN 1952 AN ENGLISH TEENAGE BOY was suffering from ichthyosis, a rare condition in which the skin is very dry, scaly, and darker than normal. The disease, commonly called "fish skin" disease, left the boy hideously disfigured on almost all of his body. No cure is known for the condition, but lubricants and oils are often prescribed to help moisten the skin and alleviate the discomfort. Dr. Albert A. Mason at the Queen Victoria Hospital in East Grinstead, Sussex, tried putting the boy into a hypnotic trance and telling him that his condition would be relieved. A few days later new skin began to grow on the boy's arm. Several further hypnotic sessions helped the boy to grow sufficient skin to be able to lead a normal life. While he was never completely cured, the marked improvement in the boy's condition made medical history.

In addition to skin problems, hypnosis has been used to help cases of asthma, allergies, hay fever, anorexia, dyspepsia, migraine, colitis, and peptic ulcers.

Although most people think of hypnotherapy as an aid to reducing, or giving up tobacco or alcohol, many are not aware that the techniques are being used seriously for the treatment of illnesses as well.

In addition to skin problems, hypnosis has been used to help treat cases of asthma, allergies, hay fever, anorexia, dyspepsia, migraine, colitis, and peptic ulcers. Hypnosis is also reportedly useful in obstetrics and gynecology. For example, in 1986 a team of English doctors helped a woman aged 37 to give birth normally even though she had lost five babies in previous deliveries. She underwent hypnosis regularly for 17 weeks prior to the birth.

MENTAL MAGIC
Hypnotic suggestion can actually lead to physiological changes in body functions. Mind over body effects include the following:

◆ Stomach contractions due to hunger can be eliminated if a person is hypnotized and told they have eaten a large meal.

◆ In a hypnotic trance, the heartbeat can be made faster or slower and the amount of blood circulating to any limb can be increased.

◆ Nearsighted people can be hypnotized to change the shape of their eyeballs and so improve their distance vision for a short time.

◆ When subjects are in a deeply hynotized state, even the tendon reflex that makes a leg jump when there is a tap on the knee is eliminated.

HYPNOSIS AND FREUD

Modern psychoanalysis, as pioneered by Sigmund Freud, owes much to early experiments probing the unconscious mind through hypnotic trance.

*I*N 1885 SIGMUND FREUD became interested in Jean-Martin Charcot's use of hypnotism with patients who had nervous diseases. During the next few years, Freud began his own private practice and used hypnosis a great deal. He treated patients who had a variety of symptoms, from painful legs to chilly feelings, depressed moods, and hallucinations. Freud's methods often involved re-enacting highly stressful experiences under hypnosis — with the patient expressing emotion in an uninhibited way.

The procedure was called "abreaction" and was a forerunner of psychoanalytical techniques. Although Freud achieved good

"I soon dropped the practice of making tests to show the degree of hypnosis reached...this roused the patients' resistance."

results through the use of hypnosis, he realized that not every patient would go into a trance, and even those patients who did respond were not permanently cured by the experience.

As Freud said: "I soon dropped the practice of making tests to show the degree of hypnosis reached, since in quite a number of cases this roused the patients' resistance and shook their confidence in me.

"Furthermore, I soon began to tire of issuing assurances and commands such as 'You are going to sleep!' and hearing 'But, doctor, I'm *not* asleep' from the patient." Freud became disillusioned with hypnosis mainly because it seemed too authoritarian and

Sigmund Freud (top) and his consulting room (above)

encouraged dependency on the part of the patient. He felt hypnosis could relieve symptoms but did nothing to help a patient understand the cause of the problem. Instead, Freud began developing the technique that he was to become famous for, which is now known by the label "psychoanalysis." The method relies on encouraging a subject to relax, concentrate, and communicate their thoughts freely and without reservation. No hypnotic trance is used.

Magnetic passions

Despite the fact that Freud stopped using hypnosis, he acknowledged that: "The importance of hypnotism for the history of the development of psychoanalysis must not be estimated too lightly."

However, Freud was concerned that hypnotic subjects frequently developed a compelling and often embarrassing "magnetic passion" for the hypnotist. One of his early

Hypnotized subjects frequently developed a compelling and often embarrassing "magnetic passion" for the hypnotist.

patients gratefully threw her arms around his neck when she was relieved of severe pain after a hypnotic session. The incident gave Freud first-hand experience of "transference" — the condition which results in a patient transferring the intense feelings of hostility or love for which they are undergoing treatment into their relationship with their therapist.

In *Group Psychology and the Analysis of the Ego* (1922), Freud drew a wider parallel between hypnosis and the experience of falling in love: "In hypnosis there is the same humble subjection, the same compliance, the same absence of criticism towards the hypnotist as towards the loved object."

Hypnosis has also been used to relieve pain during surgical operations. One dramatic example of this technique features Ukrainian Anatoly Kashpirovsky, who had worked in obscurity in a mental hospital for 25 years before suddenly becoming famous in 1988, when his penetrating eyes were shown on television screens. In front of a television audience, he used hypnotic suggestion to make a surgical operation thousands of miles away pain-free. In 1989, Kashpirovsky held five further sessions on Ukrainian television. Thousands of people came in person to attend the televised treatments, both in Moscow and Kiev. Kashpirovsky's efforts produced a flood of letters from viewers. People wrote to say they had been cured from disorders as varied as enuresis (incontinence) to psoriasis (a skin disease). Some viewers reported that their epileptic fits had become much rarer and shorter. Others claimed that their ulcers had healed, polyps were disappearing, and some diabetics seemed not to need their medicine. These claims were all made by letter and, unfortunately, were not subject to independent verification.

Patient power
Kashpirovsky believes that each person possesses a self-regulating system that can combat disease, and that the therapist does not impose his or her will on the patient, but uses influence to help them to develop their own healing powers.

In their desperate search for a cure for cancer, researchers have turned to the possible healing powers of hypnosis as a potential life-saver. In 1982 Los Angeles psychologist Bernauer W. Newton published

Anatoly Kashpirovsky

the results of his experiments that studied the use of hypnosis with 287 terminally ill cancer patients. The survival rate of those who dropped out after fewer than 10 sessions was only one-third of those who stayed the whole course. Of particular interest was a sub-group of 24 patients who received hypnosis treatment, but no conventional medical therapy for cancer. At least nine of these sufferers were found to be in spontaneous remission from their cancers.

Newton believes that deep hypnosis that is frequently repeated produces "an extremely deep state of calm." He suspects that it is the resulting state of "profound inner quiet" that helps the patient's psychological balance to return to normal, and this aids healing.

Other practitioners agree with Newton's findings. In 1976, Paul Balson of the Letterman Army Medical Center, San Francisco, described hypnotherapy as "a genuine tool for reducing anxiety." This aspect of hypnotherapy has resulted in its further use, not only in the direct treatment of cancer, but also in relieving the side effects of conventional cancer treatments. And in 1988, researcher L. G. Walker and his colleagues at the University of Aberdeen, Scotland, published a report in the *British Journal of Experimental and Clinical Hypnosis* on trials they had carried out, which showed impressive reductions in incidents of nausea, vomiting and other unpleasant symptoms that are associated with chemotherapy.

In 1982 Howard R. Hall, a psychologist at Pennsylvania State University, published a paper that described his team's research findings

> ## Kashpirovsky believes that each person possesses a self-regulating system that can combat disease.

Milton Erickson

WILL TO WALK
Psychiatrist Milton Erickson (1901–80) encouraged the use of hypnosis in psychotherapy as a result of his own experiences. The son of a Wisconsin farmer, Erickson became paralyzed by polio at the age of 17.

One day, Erickson was strapped in his rocking chair, but wished he were nearer to the window. He noticed that after he wished this, the chair began to rock. In the months that followed, Erickson practiced a kind of self-hypnosis to regain movement. Soon he became stronger and within a year, young Erickson had managed to walk with crutches. Eventually he walked unaided.

Trance relief
Erickson often used hypnosis with his terminally ill patients. For example, he taught one woman dying of cancer to develop numbness in her body. As a result she was able to have a minimum of drugs to relieve pain, allowing her to stay conscious and remain in contact with her family.

Remarkable recovery
Dr. Dabney Ewin and burn victim Jerry Baggett study a series of photographs that recorded Baggett's progress while he was undergoing successful treatment using hypnosis.

> We may not understand the basis of hypnosis, but years of experience and research show that it can work.

on "Hypnosis and the Immune System: A Review Offering Implications for Cancer and the General Psychology of Healing." Hall and his colleagues have made much use of imagery and guided visualizations, which seem to be just as effective as spoken suggestions with hypnotized subjects.

One of Hall's findings was that hypnotizable subjects can exercise an almost immediate influence on their white blood cells (lymphocytes). As some lymphocytes are crucial to the body's immune system, increasing their number helps to protect against the development of tumors.

Conquering burns

Dr. Dabney Ewin took his first course in hypnosis in 1962, and eight years later became the founding president of the New Orleans Society of Clinical Hypnosis. Dr. Ewin has discovered the value of hypnosis as treatment for a variety of problems — from hypertension

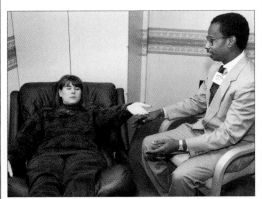

Positive thought
Howard R. Hall helps a patient to stimulate her body's immune system.

to peptic ulcers. He also treats burns patients through hypnosis. He reports most success in cases when he is able to reach the patient within two hours of the time of injury, before the "inflammatory response" has set in. Dr. Ewin claims that he blocks this response and greatly reduces recovery time.

The value of hypnosis in treating burns patients was demonstrated over 100 years ago. In 1887 a Belgian hypnotist named Joseph Delboeuf branded a subject on both arms with a red-hot iron. He told the brave patient that she would feel pain in only the left arm. It seems incredible, but the woman did indeed report pain in only the left arm. Her right arm showed no sign of swelling or inflammation following the branding.

A burning sensation

In 1975 Donald W. Schafer of the University of California, Irvine, reported on the use of hypnosis with 20 severely burned patients. Fourteen of the subjects benefited from the control of pain, especially during changes of dressing. That same year, French hypnotist Leon Chertok showed that burns could be created as well as helped by hypnosis. He filmed an experiment during which he produced a large blister on a volunteer's arm. Chertok had placed a cool coin on the arm and suggested by hypnosis that the coin was hot. The subject reported feeling no pain at all.

Lewis Thomas, one of America's leading biologists and a former director of the Memorial Sloan-Kettering Cancer Center in New York City, wrote an essay entitled "On Warts." He found it astonishing that some warts could be made to disappear by the power of thought alone, and concluded that there must be "a kind of superintelligence that exists in each of us, infinitely smarter and possessed of technical know-how far beyond our present understanding."

Non-authoritarian style

Hypnosis has developed various styles. The original authoritarian approach uses direct spoken suggestion. The more recent non-authoritarian style relies on imagination and on the subject's doing more of the work. The subject's power is as impressive as the therapist's. Whatever technique is employed, it seems clear that, through the use of hypnosis, we can activate the "superintelligence" referred to by Thomas, sometimes with immediate and extremely dramatic results. We may not understand the basis of hypnosis, but years of experience and research show that it can work.

POWER OF SUGGESTION

"I wondered why I didn't feel much pain and how I healed so quickly."

*I*N THE EARLY 1970's Jerry Baggett was rushed to the emergency room of Touro Infirmary, New Orleans, blackened skin hanging from his arms and hands. He was so badly burned following an explosion in the boiler room of the YMCA where he was chief engineer, that he wanted to die. Dr. Dabney Ewin, a surgeon at the hospital, used hypnosis to stop the pain and speed up the healing process.

Baggett expected to be scarred for life, but today he has no scars. He was back at work at the YMCA just 14 days after the accident happened.

Baggett had worked at a hospital and knew the physical and emotional pain affecting burn victims. He had also been burned twice as a young boy.

"Dr. Dabney Ewin came to me right away," Baggett reported. "He spoke very softly and was kind and consoling. He took charge and assured me that with his new method I would be OK and as good as new."

Baggett didn't realize that medical hypnosis was being used, but he recalls feeling little or no pain throughout his stay in the hospital. "I wondered why I didn't feel much pain and how I healed so quickly. It was later that Dr. Ewin explained to me that he used hypnosis in order to stop the pain and speed up the healing process."

Pain-free recovery

The expected hospital stay for someone like Baggett with deep second-degree burns on his face should have been about six weeks. Second-degree burns cause terrible blisters, and usually result in painful swelling. With facial burns of this severity, the patient would normally be unable to open his or her eyes after 24 hours. But Baggett's eyes never became swollen shut, and he didn't have the temporarily disfiguring "moon face" typical of victims with that kind of burn. Nor did he require any of the heavy medication that is usually prescribed for burn pain.

Besides being released much sooner than was usual, Baggett required only a single aspirin for a headache on the seventh day of his hospitalization. Recovery was truly remarkable, and Baggett's gratitude to Dr. Ewin and the hospital staff is understandable. "I have read many books on hypnosis since," said Baggett, "and I see all the good it can do in the proper hands of a physician dedicated to serving humanity."

For grateful patients like Jerry Baggett of New Orleans, the mystery of why hypnosis works is less important than the reality that it does.

HYPNOSIS IN SURGERY

How many people would be willing to have a tooth pulled without anesthetic? As for undergoing major surgery without conventional pain controls, the idea is too dreadful to contemplate. Yet prior to the introduction of chloroform and ether in the 1840's, such operations were frequent.

HYPNOSIS WAS FIRST USED as an anesthetic in France, where the earliest documented case was carried out in 1829. A French surgeon named Jules Cloquet removed the breast of a 69-year-old woman who had been put to "mesmeric sleep" about an hour before the operation. She showed no signs of being in pain and yet was conscious enough to talk with the surgeon while he worked.

The first recorded use of hypnosis to create a kind of surgical anesthesia in the United States was in Boston in 1836. A 12-year-old girl, Louisa, had her decayed molar extracted by a Dr. Harwood. The young patient was aware of what was happening but reported no pain. Two years later, hypnoanesthesia was used in England by Dr. John Elliotson for an operation on the

Tooth pulling
In 1836, a Frenchman, Dr. Oudet, extracted a tooth after putting his patient into a trance.

neck of a 19-year-old girl. One of the first reported major operations in England was in 1842, when W. Squire Ward amputated a man's leg at the thigh. There was much hostility to hypnoanesthesia from many doctors in Britain, and in 1843 Dr. Elliotson published a defense called "Numerous Cases of Surgical Operations Without Pain in the Mesmeric State."

Innovative attitudes

Doctors in America were not as opposed to the new technique as their British counterparts. Most early American hypnoanesthesia involved dental patients, but it was not long before the methods were tried on more serious operations. In 1843 an 18-year-old girl in Illinois reportedly had a tumor on the left side of her face painlessly removed; in 1844 a Maine surgeon amputated a leg; in 1845 a Georgia doctor removed the cancerous right breast of a 47-year-old woman.

Meanwhile, in the late 1840's, a Scottish surgeon named James Esdaile reported on his use of hypnosis in surgery in India. He claimed to have performed over 315 major and several thousand minor operations using hypnosis as the only form of anesthetic. One result was a sharp fall in post-operative infections — from 50 percent to 5 percent. Esdaile's procedures may have helped reduce anxiety and fear, however, but some patients did show signs of pain. A commission of the Bengal government concluded that Esdaile's surgery was not as successful as he claimed. Yet while patients showed signs of pain, such as moaning and

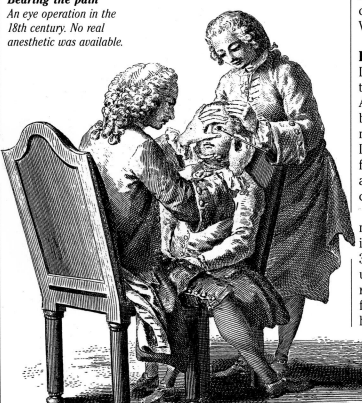

Bearing the pain
An eye operation in the 18th century. No real anesthetic was available.

grimacing, they denied having suffered when questioned after the operation.

Despite disapproval from some medical people, the use of hypnosis in surgery afforded a degree of relief at a time when surgery was very risky and usually extremely painful. The discovery of anesthetic drugs caused a decline in mesmeric surgery, but there has been renewed interest since about 1930. With the availability of modern painkillers, it may seem that hypnosis no longer has a role. But some doctors think that using the power of suggestion on the unconscious mind is still worthwhile if it lessens reliance on drugs.

In 1990, doctors at two Glasgow hospitals studied 63 women having hysterectomies. While half the women were under anesthetic, soothing messages were piped into the stereo earphones they wore. The 15-minute tapes stated: "Everything is going well; we are very pleased with your progress. You feel warm, comfortable, calm and relaxed. Any pain that you feel after the operation will not concern you."

When the women patients awoke after surgery, they were allowed to administer morphine as needed to kill their pain. The women who had heard the message needed, on average, one quarter less drugs.

Hypnosis may have a similar effect to drugs but it operates quite differently. Drugs consist of a chemical anesthetic that blocks painful impulses before they reach the brain — while hypnosis, it appears, convinces the brain to ignore the impulses.

Hypnosis is decidely not sleep, even though it may appear to be much the same. Reflexes that disappear during sleep can be elicited in the hypnotic state. Patients under hypnoanesthesia may show no overt sign of pain, but their pulse rate and blood pressure do fluctuate greatly during an operation. In addition, readings of brain rhythms confirm that hypnotized people are physiologically awake. These effects show that a hypnotic trance is indeed different from normal repose. Patients obviously feel something, but the mind is somehow mitigating the normal response to pain.

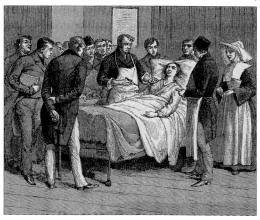

Leg amputation in the 18th century

Bedside manner
The earliest recorded use of hypnosis as an anesthetic was in 1829 when French surgeon Jules Cloquet put a 69-year-old woman to "mesmeric sleep" before an operation for breast cancer.

Going under
Hypnotist Jean-Pierre Catalifaud puts a 22-year-old patient into a deep trance before an operation to rectify a deviation in the nasal canal.

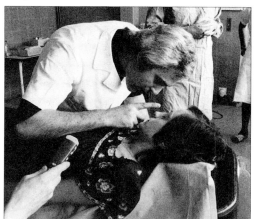

Smooth operation
Prof. Serge Plot, the surgeon, working during the 20-minute operation. The patient remained hypnotized throughout and experienced no pain.

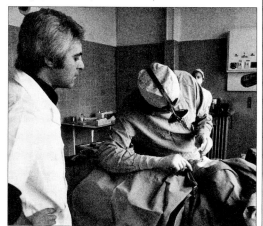

MULTIPLE
PERSONALITY

Hypnosis has been valuable for exploring the mysterious disturbance in which one person appears to have sub-personalities, sometimes hostile toward each other.

ONE DAY IN THE 1890's, a young woman named Sally took a trip into the New England countryside. She collected an assortment of snakes and spiders in a box, which she wrapped and sent to a Miss Christine Beauchamp. The recipient was terrified when she opened the box, and the creatures promptly scattered all over her room. This was typical of practical jokes played by Sally against Christine.

These were no ordinary pranks between acquaintances, however. Sally and Christine were one and the same person, an unfortunate victim of the psychological condition known as dissociation, or multiple personality.

Coexisting beings

It may be revealing that many reported cases of multiple personality date from between 1840 and 1910, when strange behavior patterns could no longer be explained away as a matter of possession by demons. Psychoanalytical ideas were not yet generally

---

The most reasonable explanation at the time was that a subject might temporarily take on a completely different personality.

---

developed and accepted. Thus the most reasonable explanation at the time was that a subject might temporarily take on a completely different personality.

Dr. Ralph Allison, author of *Minds in Many Pieces* published in 1980, described cases in which voices speaking through hypnotized patients claimed to be those of invading spirits. With dissociation, or multiple personality, it is not unusual for at least one sub-personality to be sharply contrasted to the patient's normal self and to behave like a totally different being.

Before Sigmund Freud's exposition of the unconscious mind, many doctors used the idea of dissociation to explain neurotic symptoms. Doctors believed that each personality could in turn act as if it were in charge of the body and conscious mind. These additional personalities might be aware or unaware of

others present within the same body. Psychologists today reserve the term dissociation mainly for cases where the subject takes on, for some considerable time, certain characteristics that seem particularly disconnected from the usual self.

In the case of Christine Beauchamp, her dissociation was discovered when she went to Tufts University Medical Center seeking treatment for nervous exhaustion. Dr. Morton Prince attempted to cure her by conventional means. When this failed, he tried hypnosis. Eventually he claimed that he could identify four distinct personalities, with the Sally character being the most domineering.

Joanne Woodward
Star of the film The Three Faces Of Eve.

Dr. Prince set about putting the woman together again. Using hypnotic suggestion, he joined the various sub-personalities until he obtained what he hoped to be her original character. Dr. Prince believed that the self is not a simple unit but rather a larger entity achieved by integrating several personalities. According to Dr. Prince, problems arise when a person does not manage to integrate these in a satisfactory way.

In 1957 a best-selling book, *The Three Faces of Eve,* brought the strange subject of multiple personality to a wider public. The book was written by two Georgia psychiatrists, Dr. Corbett H. Thigpen and Dr. Hervey M. Cleckley. Eve's three personalities included the inhibited Eve White, a fun-loving and flirtatious Eve Black, and Jane, who acted as a kind of referee between the other selves.

Eve's story had a happy ending in the book, but the real Eve, Chris Sizemore, then published her own, reportedly more accurate, account called *I'm Eve.* She revealed that more than three personalities were involved and that the cure described by the psychiatrists had brought her only temporary relief from the condition. Chris Sizemore believed that she was able to display several different personalities simultaneously, but in some cases one personality seemed to replace another completely. For example, in 1887 a 61-year-old preacher from Rhode Island named Ansel Bourne disappeared suddenly without trace. Two weeks later a man named A. J. Brown rented a storeroom in Pennsylvania and started a small retail business. He ran this for six weeks without arousing any suspicion. Then one morning, A. J. Brown awoke in terror and demanded to know where he was. He insisted to his bewildered landlord that his name was Ansel Bourne. The eminent psychologist William James hypnotized the man, and Bourne was able to explain in detail how A. J. Brown came to be in Pennsylvania.

Rev. W. F. Prince

Researchers have discovered that many patients suffering from dissociation have experienced some deep shock early in their lives. In 1892, little Doris Fischer was only three years old when her drunken father snatched her from her mother's arms and flung

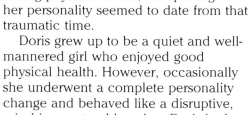

her to the floor. While she suffered no lasting physical effects, the splitting of her personality seemed to date from that traumatic time.

Doris grew up to be a quiet and well-mannered girl who enjoyed good physical health. However, occasionally she underwent a complete personality change and behaved like a disruptive, mischievous troublemaker. Doris had no knowledge of being under the influence of this secondary personality, who liked to be called Margaret. Meanwhile, the latter was aware of Doris's existence and was determined to make life difficult for her.

Sick Doris

When Doris was age 17, her mother died suddenly and life at home became barely tolerable. A third personality, "sick Doris," had appeared by then. Margaret became annoyed at sick Doris's presence and showed her aggression toward her by forcing Doris to hit and scratch herself in a vicious way until she bled.

In great distress, Doris decided to attend a church close to her home. At the new church Rev. Walter Franklin Prince and his wife noted Doris's unhappiness and encouraged her to visit them regularly. Rev. Prince was a qualified psychologist as well as a minister, and by coincidence, his doctoral thesis at Yale University had been entitled "Multiple Personality." He soon realized that such a case had landed on his doorstep.

The Princes adopted Doris, enabling Rev. Prince to study her behavior closely. After three years of using extensive direct suggestion, Rev. Prince appeared to banish the last of her other disruptive personalities. But Rev. Prince died in 1934, and without his continued treatment and support Doris went into decline and spent the rest of her unfortunate life in a mental institution.

Doris

Doris underwent a complete personality change and behaved like a mischievous troublemaker. She had no knowledge of this secondary personality, who liked to be called Margaret.

Margaret

CAPTIVATING
TALENTS

Watching someone being hypnotized can be highly entertaining. Early public demonstrations became part of show business as hypnotists traveled from Europe to America in the early 1800's to work. These performers created interest in the alternative uses of their art.

A N OUTSTANDING EUROPEAN hypnotist-showman who traveled to the United States in the 19th century was Carl Hansen, a Dane. He used hypnosis to produce effects such as amnesia, insensitivity to pain, and assorted hallucinations. The highlight of his show was to induce total cataleptic rigidity in a volunteer who was stretched between two chairs, supported only at the head and feet. Such displays became extremely popular with stage hypnotists over the next century.

Hypnotists like Hansen awakened the interest of doctors but frightened off many potential patients. Audiences watched unsuspecting volunteers performing trivial or even embarrassing acts on the stage at the hypnotist's bidding. As a result, many ordinary people feared a visit to even a highly qualified practitioner.

Posthypnotic suggestion is one of the most curious features of hypnotism. As researcher Martin T. Orne of the University of Pennsylvania points out: "A deeply hypnotized individual, instructed during hypnosis that at some later time he will carry out an item of behavior in response to a specific cue, will tend to do so, often without awareness that he is carrying out a hypnotist's suggestion."

Boosting chances
American tennis star Arthur Ashe has been one of a number of sports figures using posthypnotic suggestion to help them play well.

> # Just as the effects of hypnosis can be extended into the future by means of posthypnotic suggestion, so it is possible to probe backward in time.

Just as the effects of hypnosis can be extended into the future by means of posthypnotic suggestion, so it is possible to probe backward in time. Subjects may be guided, or "regressed," not only back to birth, but even beyond to what may seem to be a previous life. These earlier lives may be described in compelling detail and the subject may adopt the identity of a totally different person while in a hypnotic trance. But although the responses of regressed subjects seem convincing, researchers suggest that these fascinating identities should not be accepted as evidence of authentic "previous lives."

British hypnotist Leonard Wilder had the intriguing idea of regressing the same people twice, with a break of several years between sessions. All the subjects produced other-life memories. Some of the memories produced in the second regression were similar but far from identical to those produced the first time. In some cases, the responses were quite different the second time.

Similar caution was suggested by Martin T. Orne following his analysis of a study of hypnotic regression carried out at the Harvard University Psychology Clinic, the results of which were published in a 1951 issue of the *Journal of Abnormal Psychology*. During the study subjects were supposedly regressed to the age of six. Drawings by these age-regressed subjects showed a mixture of childlike and mature characteristics. Such inconsistencies in their "six-year-old" behavior showed that their personalities remained adult and that the regression was not complete.

However incomplete it may be, hypnotic regression does appear to have some value in psychotherapy as a way of uncovering traumatic experiences, both real and imaginary. It is also thought by some to be an invaluable aid to crime detection. For example, an eyewitness to a bank robbery may be hypnotized to remember the license number of a car. Unfortunately, such information can be completely inaccurate. Hypnotized people, in fact, may "remember" events that never took place, especially if they are asked leading questions.

Misleading trance

Such "false memory" was demonstrated in the late 19th century by a French hypnotist named Jules Liegeois. He persuaded a woman in a deep hypnotic trance that she had witnessed a major crime. Liegeois then arranged for a lawyer friend to interrogate the woman,

ANIMAL REACTIONS

Animals employ hypnotic techniques and sometimes "bewitch" their prey. Small birds, hares, and even antelopes may be lulled into a rigid state, allowing the attacker to gain control.

Egyptian snake charmers apply pressure on the back of a cobra's neck to put the creature into a hypnotic state. The snake then becomes rigid, as in the cataleptic hypnotic state, rising out of the basket like a stick.

A Hindu snake charmer

You can bewitch a frog by laying it belly-up on the palm of your hand. Lightly tap its belly with your other hand, or just snap your fingers over it a few times. The frog will then stay immobile for hours, until you awaken it by tapping its belly again.

Hypnosis is used widely in the U.S.A. and Britain to change behavior and eradicate unwanted habits. Therapists say it takes from three to five sessions to stop smoking or to start losing weight – while other problems may require 5 to 10 sessions. Some of the other problems that hypnosis attempts to relieve are: accident proneness, carsickness, lack of confidence, frustration, feelings of inferiority, learning difficulties, poor memory, nail biting, nightmares, panic, poor public speaking, seasickness, shyness, stage fright.

Alcoholic cure
Hypnosis is being used to help alcoholics in the U.S.S.R. become less dependent on drink.

posing as a judge investigating the imaginary crime. The woman gave all the facts to the lawyer and was even willing to testify in court under oath. Liegeois then hypnotized the woman again, removing the false memories that he had implanted earlier.

In a 1980 murder case in Joliet, Illinois, a man was brought to trial largely on the evidence provided by a hypnotized eyewitness. The subject was acquitted, however, as soon as it was learned that the key witness had been nearly 100 yards from the crime and that street lighting had been poor.

Strange encounters

Enterprising researchers are constantly finding new areas for the use of hypnosis. In 1977 Alvin H. Lawson, a professor of English at California State University, Long Beach, startled delegates at a congress on unidentified flying objects (UFO's) by announcing the surprising results of some highly original experiments.

Sixteen volunteers with no experience of UFO's were hypnotized. Before they were questioned by Lawson, none of these people claimed any knowledge of UFO's, let alone any encounter with a spacecraft. Lawson took them through a typical abduction experience, before asking them the kinds of questions he would have asked people who believed they had been contacted by aliens. He was surprised to receive detailed narratives which were virtually the same as those given by people who claimed to have been abducted.

Lawson concluded that a UFO encounter experience was simply "an involuntary, fantasized sequence of images and events unconsciously based on perinatal or birth memories." And there are in fact numerous similarities between the memories of those who think they have been abducted by aliens and images of the womb.

Birth memories

In addition, Lawson noted that people born by cesarean section did not describe the usual tunnel imagery in their hypnotically induced memories of contact with UFO's. One particular subject whose birth had been forceps-

UFO investigator Alvin H. Lawson

aided described being "pulled on board" a spacecraft. Another subject, who had been born in a breech position, claimed to have exited the UFO by "sinking to the ground seated." Lawson found that the more detailed the description of a close encounter with a UFO, the more perinatal data was included.

Use of hypnosis has led to the theory that all claimed encounters with UFO's are in fact memories of birth. Yet it does seem possible that hypnotized subjects may be regressed to the start of life and may produce an accurate description of it. There also appears to be some scientific basis to the concept of self awareness before and during birth. The July 20, 1984, issue of *Science* magazine, for example, featured research showing that fetuses can learn in the womb.

Mutual trance

What are the limits of hypnosis? No one knows for sure. An intriguing experiment in 1962 hinted at possible further developments. Psychologist Charles T. Tart of the University of California tried an experiment to deepen the level of hypnotic trance. He arranged for two subjects, Bill and Anne, to hypnotize each other. Bill began the unusual experiment by inducing hypnosis in Anne. He suggested that she concentrate on her breathing, that her eyes would close and she would see a blue vapor flowing in and out of her nostrils. She was told she would feel herself falling backward into hypnosis.

After the session Anne reported that she had felt herself falling backward as she went into a trance. She described the experience as the hypnotic trance

HYPNOSIS AND CRIME

For over a century, the use of hypnosis to help clarify the memories of victims and witnesses of crime has been highly controversial.

IN 1976 MARTIN REISER, director of the Los Angeles Police Department's Behavioral Science Services, established new four-day training courses, during which police officers were taught to use hypnosis as part of their investigative techniques.

Reiser believed that hypnosis is a safe way of eliciting memories that are difficult to uncover by standard

The driver remembered little when interviewed normally, but a vital clue emerged under hypnosis.

interview procedures. According to Reiser, much useful information lies in the depths of the human mind.

However, Reiser recognizes the problem of confabulation, the psychologist's term for the tendency of a hypnotized person to fill in memory gaps with fantasized material which the subject believes is true. However, he does not think this risk should hinder police from employing the technique.

One example of the successful use of hypnosis in law enforcement took place in California in 1976, when a school bus was hijacked with children on board. The 55-year-old driver remembered little when interviewed normally, but a vital clue emerged under hypnosis. He was able to tell police the last five letters and digits of the license plate on the van used by the criminals.

In the late 1970's and early 1980's, New York City's Police Department Hypnosis Unit used hypnosis in over 400 cases. The unit said that hypnosis provided significant new information in three-quarters of these crimes.

Despite such reported successes, the Society for Clinical and Experimental Hypnosis and the International Society

of Hypnosis have been critical of police department use of the technique. These organizations argue that the police training is inadequate, and that police may inadvertently convey their own feelings as to who is guilty.

Vital witness
Dr. Martin Reiser questions a hypnotized witness, while a police artist interprets her recollections.

American courts were at first reluctant to admit evidence that was elicited through hypnosis. Then, in 1968, the Maryland Court of Special Appeals ruled that hypnotically elicited testimony could be admitted as evidence in a rape trial. The judge emphasized that the testimony should be corroborated by other evidence.

Inadmissable evidence
During the 1970's a number of courts followed this Maryland ruling. However, a 1982 decision from the same Maryland court said that while hypnosis could be used to obtain information to help the police, hypnotic memories were inadmissible as evidence in court. Meanwhile, other courts have ruled differently, and the debate is likely to continue. American states have legislated in different ways, and Great Britain as yet has no formal legislation governing the use of hypnotically induced testimony. France has prohibited such testimony in court.

Self-hypnosis cassettes
Self-hypnosis cassettes to help people deal with a variety of problems are now available.

FEAR OF FLYING
Millions of people suffer from a fear of flying. Self-hypnosis cassettes are being marketed to work on the subconscious, by combining gentle relaxation techniques with positive thinking. These tapes, designed to relieve the sufferer's anxiety, can be played at home before a flight, in the departure lounge, or even during takeoff.

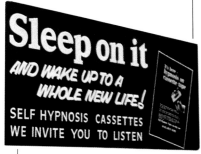

HYPNOTISM IN THE MOVIES
The association of hypnosis with charlatans, stage entertainers, and movie villains using the power for their own ends has not encouraged public confidence in the technique. Hypnotherapists today emphasize that they do not impose their will on the patient. Hypnosis is instead a way of revealing to a patient what his or her own mind can accomplish.

Donald Wolfit as the wicked Svengali

Evil manipulator
Svengali was the 1954 film version of George du Maurier's novel *Trilby*, which was set in Paris in 1894. After being hypnotized by the evil Svengali, cabaret singer Trilby becomes a great singer. The man she truly loves sees her at a concert, but she does not recognize him. Svengali sees the young man, has a fit of jealous hatred, and dies from a heart attack. This releases Trilby from her trance, with no memory of her singing triumphs, or of Svengali's power over her.

Trilby becomes weaker. One day she sees a photograph of Svengali and stares into the "big black eyes full of stern command." She begins to sing and falls back on her pillow, whispering Svengali's name as she dies.

Acting strangely
The illustration shows the strange case of an actress who was hypnotized during an evening performance on a French stage in 1904. An actor playing the part of a hypnotist made fake "magnetic passes" over the cast. Actors and audience alike were amazed when one young actress suddenly went into a trance. She stayed entranced until the early hours of the next morning.

deepened: "I had a sensation for the first time of actually relinquishing control. I had a most unusual physical sensation of my body disintegrating — with great chunks falling off like thick bark on a tree. I was momentarily threatened, almost resisted, reassured myself, and soon this feeling passed, after which my body was *gone*, and I felt like a *soul* or a big ball of *mind*."

Once Anne was entranced, Bill instructed her to hypnotize him. This she did by holding up a finger and telling him to watch it closely. After Bill's eyes closed, Anne closed hers and began describing how they were climbing down a manhole together. She said that they would be deeply hypnotized by the time they reached the bottom.

Anne spoke of seeing bright, glowing crystals on the walls as they descended. Bill reported that he was seeing these too. The two led each other into deeper and deeper trance states in which they seemed to share hallucinations. Anne described dreaming that they were in a car in the desert, watching the road unwind, seeing small lizards on the sand, then walking along the desert road, feeling hot and sticky. Bill said he had been having the same dream.

At a second session Bill described

Dubious intentions
Hypnosis is used for immoral purposes in the movie The Hypnotist. *Such portrayals have added to public unease about losing control.*

their journey deeper and deeper into a tunnel. This seemed to be very real to them both while in the trance. After this session, the two subjects developed an intense friendship and felt close to each other as a result of their shared experience. During a third session they said they entered a heavenly place.

Fusion of identities
A heightened empathy and communication between the subjects resulted from the mutual hypnosis, like a partial fusion of identities. Anne said that sometimes they seemed to walk through each other. It was a blending of selves well beyond their normal experience. But the two subjects felt frightened at the thought of their individuality being lost, even temporarily. Anne was reluctant but willing to go on with experiments while Bill strongly resisted any more sessions. Dr. Tart was obliged to end what seemed a fascinating glimpse into an uncharted area of human consciousness.

Relative rewards
The film On a Clear Day You Can See Forever *(1970) starred Yves Montand as a hypnotherapist, and took the subject of hypnosis well into the realm of fiction. In the film a wealthy man persuades the therapist to let him glimpse his future lives, so that he can leave his fortune to himself.*

AGAINST YOUR WILL?

Can people under hypnosis be persuaded to act against their will? Professional hypnotherapists tend to say no, but the question is still open.

*S*OME EXPERIMENTAL studies suggest that hypnotized people can be made to perform acts that are immoral or harmful, either to themselves or others. These acts include such antisocial behavior as minor thefts and verbal attacks. Often subjects are willing to do what they are told because they want to help the hypnotist, or because they think their actions will be safe because the hypnotist will take responsibility for whatever results from his or her hypnotic suggestion.

Moral dilemmas

Paul Young of Indiana State University conducted some intriguing experiments in 1952. Deeply hypnotized subjects were asked to throw acid at an experimenter and to pick up a dangerous snake. (Both the experimenter and the snake were behind a plate of glass that was invisible.) The majority of subjects attempted to throw the acid and pick up the snake when hypnotized — but refused when not in the hypnotic state.

In 1947 Chicago psychologist John Watkins successfully persuaded a hypnotized army private to attack a senior officer — an offense punishable by court-martial. The private was persuaded that the officer was a dangerous enemy. It took three men to restrain the private and keep him from strangling and stabbing the officer.

Meanwhile, some experimenters claim there is a fail-safe mechanism within us that can overrule orders that go against our individual moral code. In 1972 Martin T. Orne of the University of Pennsylvania wrote in the

International Journal of Clinical and Experimental Hypnosis that: "Once hypnotized, the subject does not lose complete control over his or her actions....Hypnosis does not make it possible for a subject to be compelled to carry out behavior which is repugnant to him. Rather, research has shown that hypnosis is likely to be less effective than many other forms of social influence that may induce one individual to carry out the request of another."

For example, in 1975 researcher E. E. Levitt of the Department of Psychology, University of Indiana, reportedly found that hypnotized subjects would cut up the American flag or mutilate the Bible only if they were prepared to carry out the same acts in an unhypnotized state.

Universal impulses?

Whether or not an unscrupulous hypnotist can induce antisocial behavior is still a controversial matter. In 1972 John Watkins was working in the Department of Psychology at the University of Montana, having spent over 25 years studying hypnotic techniques. Watkins insisted that all of us harbor anti-social impulses and that there is always the possibility that any unusual "states," including those induced by drugs or alcohol, may be sufficient to release these impulses. As Watkins stated: "No method of treatment known to man is devoid of the possibility of a harming influence. A procedure strong enough to do some good is strong enough to do harm."

The limits of control
In 1807 the marquis de Puységur insisted that the authority of the mesmerist could not be abused: "I was questioning a woman in a magnetic state as to the extent of the powers that I could exercise upon her. 'I bet that if I really wanted, I could use you in any way I want, ask you to get undressed, etc....' She replied, 'You will never be able to force me to take off all of my clothes. My shoes, my hat; but beyond that, you will get nothing'...."

Puységur

NEW TECHNIQUES

The approach to hypnosis has changed markedly in recent years. While traditional hypnosis gives instructions in an authoritarian way (e.g. "You will sit down"), the modern method is much less direct. The suggestion might be "maybe your legs ache," and the hypnotist may even sit down in order to lead by example.

Increased efficiency

Psycholinguists have studied the language used in hypnosis, and this has led to more efficient methods. Hypnosis may cure a phobia in as short a time as 10 minutes. There is also an emphasis now on finding out a person's interests and skills as a help to the induction process. Another recent development is the use of hypnosis in fields such as social work. This is proving especially helpful with adults who have suffered abuse as children.

British Hypnosis Research (BHR) began exploring the subject in 1979. By 1984, BHR had established training courses for dentists, social workers, and others in the caring professions.

A modern approach
Stephen Brooks hypnotizes a patient at St. Anne's Hospital in London. Mr. Brooks is a senior instructor with British Hypnosis Research. He has developed an indirect, less authoritarian approach and also supports the wider use of hypnosis in fields such as speech therapy, counseling, and physiotherapy.

CHAPTER THREE

POWERS OF PERCEPTION

Since early times there have been individuals who could apparently sense things that were beyond the abilities of others. In some cultures such people were revered, but in many societies those with inexplicable sensitivities were feared, and sometimes killed.

The relentless progress in science and technology has done nothing to erode the widespread belief in paranormal powers. Rich and poor alike seek guidance from clairvoyants who claim that they can "see" into the future and "know" what course of action is right for their clients. Judging the accuracy of psychic readings is almost impossible — people tend to remember only what comes true and not to remember all the leading questions the clairvoyant may have used to extract information.

ACCURATE REPRODUCTIONS

In the 1920's novelist Upton Sinclair and his wife, Mary, became amateur psychical researchers. Mary claimed success at telepathically reproducing unknown images drawn by her husband, his secretary, and her brother-in-law. In one early experiment, the brother-in-law drew a picture of a fork while at a location 40 miles away. Meanwhile, Mary applied her concentration to reading his mind and reportedly wrote down: "See a table fork. Nothing else."

Upton and Mary Sinclair

Friends of the Sinclairs were critical of their interest in psychic matters, and a newspaper article carried the title "Sinclair Goes Spooky." Sinclair defended the research and his conclusions: "I don't like to believe in telepathy, because I don't know what to make of it. I would rather give all my time to my muck-raking job [as a writer exposing social injustice]. The conviction has been forced upon me that telepathy is real, and loyalty to the nature of the universe makes it necessary for me to say so."

Many ordinary people are convinced that they too have a sixth sense, one that they use spontaneously in their everyday lives. Some well-known business people attribute their success to such a sixth sense, and believe that it enables them to make the right "seat-of-the-pants" decisions at crucial stages in their careers. All of which has encouraged scientists to give the ability a name — extrasensory perception (ESP) — and to search for proof of its existence within the confines of the laboratory.

A devastating prediction

One of the earliest ESP experiments is said to have been conducted by King Croesus of Lydia (who ruled from 560 to 546 B.C.), to test the abilities of the Greek oracles. Croesus wanted to go to war with one of this neighbors, and according to Greek author Herodotus, who recorded the story, he decided to consult an oracle about the outcome of the conflict. But how was he to know which seer was the best? His solution was to send envoys to the oracles with the greatest reputations and have them ask: "What is the King of Lydia doing today?" Five oracles failed in their attempts at prediction. The sixth was nearly right. But the oracle of Apollo at Delphi, speaking through a sorceress, was correct with this reply: "I can count the sands, and I can measure the ocean; I have ears for the silent, and I know what the dumb man meaneth. Lo! on my senses there striketh the smell of a shell-covered tortoise, boiling now on a fire, with the flesh of a lamb, in a cauldron. Brass is the vessel below, and brass the cover of it."

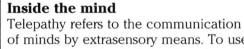

> ## "I can count the sands, and I can measure the ocean; I have ears for the silent, and I know what the dumb man meaneth...."
> **The oracle of Apollo**

The oracle of Apollo at Delphi
A 19th-century engraving.

At that very time, the king was boiling a tortoise and a lamb in a brass pot. Not surprisingly, the oracle at Delphi was chosen to advise the king on the outcome of the war, and it predicted that a great empire would be destroyed. Unfortunately, King Croesus did not ask which empire. It turned out to be his.

Extrasensory perception is a term that is used loosely to describe a whole range of paranormal phenomena. For example, if a person is able to describe a place or an event hundreds of miles away, this might be due to a number of extrasensory possibilities. They could include the following: telepathy, clairvoyance, remote viewing, or out-of-body experiences.

Inside the mind

Telepathy refers to the communication of minds by extrasensory means. To use telepathy to gather information about an independent event happening elsewhere, for example, a subject would have to communicate with the mind of someone who was witnessing it.

Among those who have claimed to be able to demonstrate telepathy at will were novelist Upton Sinclair and his wife, Mary. They claimed they could read each other's minds, and they demonstrated this ability by "sending" and "receiving" drawings to and from one another. Mrs. Sinclair believed herself to be especially psychic and acted as "receiver" of the mental images that her husband "sent" to her. The Sinclairs often seemed to do this with uncanny accuracy, sometimes from adjoining rooms and at other times over far longer distances.

In 1930 the Sinclairs published the results of their work in a book entitled *Mental Radio*. This reported a success rate of 23 percent in 290 experiments and partial successes in 53 percent of the tests. Albert Einstein had witnessed some of the Sinclairs' experiments and wrote a supportive foreword for the German edition of the book.

A visionary talent

In contrast to telepathy, clairvoyance is the talent to "see" events simply by tuning into them in some way that does not involve reading minds.

In 1958 researcher Dr. Milan Ryzl, who now lives and works in the U.S., carried out clairvoyance experiments in Czechoslovakia with a young girl named Josefka. She was hypnotized and then given sealed opaque envelopes containing Zener cards and asked to identify them. Zener cards are used to test psychic ability and consist of normal-sized cards with five different symbols on them: a circle, a square, a plus sign, wavy lines, and a star. Out of 250 guesses, Josefka was right 121 times. If chance alone had been responsible, researchers say, she might have given only 50 correct answers.

During one hypnotic test, Josefka became distressed and began describing a scene in which a girlfriend was approached by a stranger in a restaurant. Josefka saw them drive away speedily on a motorbike, then stop. She described the terrible scene as the man attacked her friend. Believing this to be a premonition, Josefka phoned her friend the next day and warned her not to accept a lift from a stranger. But it was too late; the event she had described to the researchers had reportedly happened at exactly the time she "saw" it while under hypnosis.

A research site on the island of Kerguelen

The coordinates given to Swann were for the remote island of Kerguelen in the southern Indian Ocean, 13,000 miles away.

Mind travel

Remote viewing means using the mind to "travel" consciously to a far-off place, see it, and describe it, rather than just "knowing" about it, as is apparently the case with clairvoyance. And unlike telepathy, remote viewing does not involve two individuals "transmitting" and "receiving" images, but rather consists of one person's mind "roaming" in search of information. Psychic Ingo Swann claims to possess the ability to carry out remote viewing, and several experiments featuring him are particularly well documented. During tests at the Stanford Research Institute in California, with researchers Harold Puthoff and Russell Targ in the mid-1970's, Swann was asked to "travel" in his mind to a location at latitude 49°20'S, longitude 70°14'E. Swann was not allowed to consult a map, but he began describing a rocky island with a cold climate. He said he could "see" a few buildings, one of which was orange, and some trucks. He then drew a map and spoke about certain characteristics of the island and its coastline.

Accurate description

The coordinates given to Swann were for the remote island of Kerguelen in the southern Indian Ocean, 13,000 miles away. The island is administered as part of the French Southern and Antarctic fields and is the base for a French-Soviet research project studying the upper atmosphere, hence the buildings and trucks that were

HEARING THINGS

While clairvoyance is the ability to "know" things beyond our normal experience, clairaudience is the ability to "hear" in some inexplicable way. From the age of 13, Joan of Arc heard voices that she believed foretold her future. The voices said she would lead an army against the English siege at Orléans in 1429 and that she would be wounded during the fighting; both of these predictions proved accurate. The voices also told Joan that a sword inscribed with five crosses would be found near the altar of a specific church at Fierbois. When she asked priests to look behind the altar, the sword was discovered.

St. Joan

Joan of Arc was tried and convicted of witchcraft and heresy by an English-dominated church court in 1431, and subsequently burned at the stake. Nearly 500 years later, the Catholic Church declared her a saint.

Prepared for war
This painting by French artist Lucien Lantier (b. 1879) shows Joan of Arc experiencing a vision of the armored archangel Michael.

DREAM IMAGES

Researchers believe that a high proportion of spontaneous ESP experiences happen to people when they are asleep or nearly asleep, and that people are also more likely to experience ESP at night than during the day.

In the 1960's Dr. Montague Ullman conducted early experiments into dream-ESP at the Dream Laboratory of the Maimonides Medical Center in New York. Experimenters had discovered that when people dream their eye muscles show

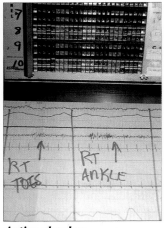

Active slumber
Monitoring equipment registers a sleeping subject's brain activity, REM, and muscle tension.

rapid eye movement (REM), and had come to the conclusion that subjects would probably be most receptive to ESP at that time. When subjects began showing REM, senders tried to use ESP to transmit pictures to them. As each burst of REM ended, the sleeper was awakened and asked about his or her dreams to see if they had received any of the images.

A number of positive results obtained over several nights suggested that dream ESP had occurred. In a second series of tests carried out over eight nights, judges decided that the dream report successfully linked with the picture on six occasions — a success rate of 75 percent. Chance alone might have produced only one successful link between the picture and the dream over eight consecutive nights.

described by Swann. Ultimately, the researchers came to the conclusion that there was little possibility that Swann would have been able to guess the details of the location so accurately, even with a good knowledge of geography.

Leaving the body

An out-of-body experience (OBE) is similar to remote viewing, in that individuals state that they are actually able to visit and see locations that are miles away. But the difference is that such individuals claim to detach their "astral bodies" from their physical bodies during sleep or a trance, leaving the astral body free to travel to the site in question and witness an event.

In 1973, tests were carried out into the nature of OBE's at the Psychical Research Foundation in Durham, South Carolina, by researchers Robert Morris, Joseph Janis, John Hartwell, and W. G. Roll. They considered the possibility that animals might be able to detect the presence of astral bodies, and they asked research assistant Stuart Harary to go into an out-of-body state and try to calm a nervous kitten. Harary was duly wired up to various monitors and attempted to separate his physical and astral bodies. While Harary was undergoing his OBE, the reactions of two kittens were watched carefully by researchers. While one kitten showed no noticeable reaction, the movement and activity of the other one calmed considerably during the times that Harary was supposedly out of his body. The researchers decided to carry out further tests with the more responsive of the kittens. When they subsequently published their results in the American Society for Psychical Research's journal,

Evelyn Adams

they noted that the kitten "responded consistently to OBE times by becoming quiet, and did so without exception."

Although it may seem unlikely, at least to supporters of psychic research, that any, or all, of these cases could be explained away as coincidence, this possibility cannot be dismissed, because the probability of coincidence is generally greater than we think. For example, if there are 23 people in a room, it is an even chance that two of them will have the same birthday. And in 1986 Mrs. Evelyn Adams of New Jersey won top prize of $1.4 million in the state lottery, just four months after scooping the $3.9 million first prize in an earlier version of the competition. The odds against such a dual win were listed at 17 trillion to one.

Same place, same time

In the 1950's conductor Pablo Casals told the story that when he was nearly 80, he took his wife-to-be, Martita (40 years his junior), to Puerto Rico, where they visited his mother's birthplace in the town of Mayaguez. As Casals recalls: "There we discovered an astonishing thing. The house in which my mother had been born in 1856 turned out to be the very same house in which Martita's mother was born some 60 years later! Not only that, but our mothers had both been born on the same day of the same month, November 13."

Pablo and Martita Casals

However strange such coincidences appear to be, they do serve to remind us that although the odds are against unlikely events happening by chance, they do indeed occur. Yet few would suggest, supporters argue, that coincidence could explain all the evidence for extrasensory perception.

Extreme States

Some researchers believe that our minds may be receiving ESP signals all the time, and that our normal, everyday activities drown them out. The result: the messages penetrate our conscious minds only in exceptional circumstances.

In the 1950's Czechoslovakian researcher Stepan Figar was the first person to investigate scientifically the possibility that ESP was more likely to occur between emotionally linked relatives. Figar separated two relatives by a screen and linked one of them to a plethysmograph, a machine that records shifts in blood volume from one part of the body to another. The other relative was then asked to make a mathematical calculation, an exercise that would normally cause blood to flow to the brain. Figar found that the relative who had not carried out the calculation showed a shift of blood to the brain at the same time, suggesting that unconscious ESP was indeed taking place.

Shifts of emotion

In 1962 researcher Dr. E. Douglas Dean who was working in the Parapsychology Foundation's research division in New York, followed up on Figar's research. Dean carried out his experiments with subjects separated by a wall, and once again a plethysmograph

Dr. E. Douglas Dean

was used to monitor blood volume changes in the subject. However, in these experiments the "sender" of information was given names written on cards, some of which had emotional significance for either the subject or the sender, while others were selected randomly from a phone book.

Every 20 seconds, the sender tried to communicate the name on a single card. An independent group of judges then compared the plethysmograph record of shifts in blood flow. The judges discovered that when emotionally meaningful names were sent, the apparatus linked to the subject recorded greater changes than at other times.

Following such seemingly positive research results, the challenge for researchers was to find ways of allowing these psychic stimuli to infiltrate the conscious mind. Thus the next logical step was to work

"The Dancing School" by Edgar Degas (1831-1917)

with altered states of consciousness, such as hypnosis, trances, and dreaming, in which psychic impressions might make more of an impact on our minds.

In the 1970's psychologist Dr. William Erwin joined forces with parapsychologist Dr. Montague Ullman in an attempt to ascertain the relationship between dreaming and ESP. During one experiment the sleeping Dr. Erwin was "sent" the image of the Degas painting "The Dancing School." When Erwin woke up he accurately described a class, a school, and "one little girl that was trying to dance with me."

Dying messages

Another altered state of consciousness that might be conducive to paranormal perceptions sometimes occurs when people are dying. Deathbed visions have been reported around the world and are often remarkably similar. Dying people sometimes report seeing a dead loved one who, they suggest, has apparently come to meet them.

In other cases, the emotions of a dying person may have an impact on the living. At age 14 Stanley Krippner, who was later to become one of America's leading psychic investigators, had set his heart on owning a set of encyclopedias. But because his parents were having a bad year, they could not afford to buy him a set. When he heard this bad news, Krippner went to his room and cried. But then he remembered his Uncle Max, who was well-off and could afford to buy him the books. How best to approach him?

Suddenly, Krippner sat bolt upright in bed: a dreadful thought had come into his mind: "Uncle Max can't help me because he's dead."

Years later Krippner commented: "At that moment, I heard the telephone ring. My mother answered the phone, then began sobbing. My cousin had told her that Max had been taken ill unexpectedly, was rushed to hospital, and had just died." Was Krippner's experience coincidence — or a case of ESP?

JUST A HUNCH?

From a strange sense of impending danger that may save a life, to an uncanny hunch about an investment that produces a fortune, many ordinary people believe that they have experienced extrasensory perception in their everyday lives.

*I*N 1979 JIM OLESAK WAS DRIVING from his home near Chicago to visit his mother in Manistique, Michigan, on her 80th birthday. He was suddenly overwhelmed by a strange feeling that someone was in terrible trouble. Inexplicably, 90 miles from his mother's home, Olesak turned off the highway and began a long detour. At the end of the lonely track was the farm of his 70-year-old cousin, Steve Hoholik. There was no reason why Olesak should be making a visit. In fact, the men had not met for 30 years.

Deserted farmhouse

When Olesak reached the farmhouse, he found the door swinging open and no one inside. He decided that Hoholik must be working somewhere on the 200 acres he farmed alone. Feeling foolish, Olesak decided to get into his car, but the strange sense of foreboding was overpowering. So Jim walked into the fields until he reached the top of a hill, a mile away. Looking down, Olesak saw Hoholik's overturned tractor and his cousin lying with his right leg trapped under one of the tractor's huge wheels. He had been there for 25 hours. Doctors said they would definitely have had to amputate Hoholik's right foot if he had been there much longer.

Steve Hoholik was immensely grateful that Olesak took the detour. "I've been wondering what brought him just when I needed help most," Hoholik said when he had recovered.

Psychic urges

Such dramatic interventions are rare. More often than not, the intrusion of ESP into everyday life may be just puzzling. In 1978 psychical researcher Rosalind Heywood explained that she believed her ESP to be so highly developed that she knew exactly when her husband would be home late from work and arranged dinner times accordingly. She described these hunches as "urges to action" or "orders." Heywood illustrated how they worked in her book *The Infinite Hive*:

"Orders said that the water should be turned off at the main as a pipe in the attic bathroom was going to burst. I knew that this irrational prediction would stand little chance with my rational husband. It looked far more like fussing than ESP. As I expected, when I told him of it, he kindly gave me the technical reasons why

EXTROVERTS AND ESP

Dr. Gertrude Schmeidler of the City University of New York began testing ESP abilities in 1942. Her experiments over a number of years have shown that people who think that there is a possibility that ESP exists tend to score better on tests than people who are not believers.

Friendly believers

Basic personality differences between believers and non-believers could be at the root of better ESP test results. Studies have shown that believers tend to be more extroverted, more friendly, and more outgoing than non-believers. As ESP involves communication between people, so it may be that an outgoing person is more likely to experience ESP than an introvert. For example, in the 1950's, researcher Betty Humphrey at Duke University reported that she had found a clear link between extroversion and ESP. In 1981 a summary of 19 ESP research reports showed that extroverts scored better than introverts in all but one of the reports.

Dr. Hans J. Eysenck

In 1967 psychologist Dr. Hans J. Eysenck advanced a theory as to why extroverts achieve better ESP test results. He hypothesized that extroverts have different alpha brain wave rhythms, showing a more relaxed, low arousal state, and that there may be some relationship between these low arousal brain waves and a capacity for ESP.

TWICE THE TALENT

Identical twins not only look alike, they frequently behave in the same way and have the same tastes. Occasionally they even marry, give birth, or die on the same day. Not surprisingly, their actions and interactions are sometimes presented as examples of extrasensory perception.

IN 1965, RESEARCHERS Dr. T. D. Duane and Dr. Thomas Behrendt from Jefferson Medical College, Philadelphia, carried out experiments with identical twins, which involved monitoring each twin's brain rhythms in separate laboratories. When a stimulus was administered to the brain of one of them, it was simultaneously received by the other, which seemed to indicate that some form of ESP was taking place.

However, when Drs. Duane and Behrendt published their results in *Science* (Vol. 150), the journal of the American Association for the Advancement of Science, the editor was rebuked by many people who refused to accept the results. In subsequent tests with 16 other pairs of twins, only one pair responded in a similar way.

As researcher Peter Watson noted in his book *Twins* (1981), it is in everyday life that the behavior of twins is most puzzling. For example, Watson described the case of Michael and Alex Chisholm who lived in Lanarkshire, Scotland, and were inseparable until the age of 17. In 1955 Michael joined the merchant navy as a cabin boy. Four days after Michael set sail for Egypt, Alex complained of tiredness and died of a heart attack. Michael was in the Bay of Biscay when he heard the news. That night, Michael died inexplicably in his sleep — less than 48 hours after his twin.

Stranger still is the story of Dorothy Collins and her twin sister Marjorie, who lived in different countries. In April 1961 Dorothy died from an accidental overdose of sleeping pills at her Brighton, England, home just a few hours before a cable arrived to tell her that her twin had died in South Africa.

It could be that these examples are no more than medical coincidences, but this does not seem to have been the case with the examination results of Nancy and Ruth Schneider of Virginia. Although the twins, who were born in 1927, took their college entrance exams in opposite corners of the classroom, they not only chose the same essay subject but also wrote word-for-word precisely the same story, according to one of the examiners.

The discovery of possible ESP in twins is sometimes incidental to other research. Such is the case with Dr. David Lykken and Dr. Thomas J. Bouchard of the University of Minnesota, who have carried out an extensive study of identical twins. They report that one pair of twins in California, Nettie and Nita, appear to have a strong telepathic link. If one girl concentrates on the other, the twin soon responds by phoning her.

Twin research has included a comparison of identical pairs who were adopted at birth and brought up by different families. One well-documented case in the University of Minnesota files concerns the "Jim twins" who met for the first time in 1979 — at the age of 39. Both boys had been named James by their adoptive parents and they discovered the following coincidences in their lives.

Parallel lives

Each Jim twin had married a girl named Linda, divorced, then married a woman named Betty. Each twin had named his first son James Alan, though one was spelled Allan. Both twins had dogs named Toy when they were boys. As adults, the Jim twins both went on vacation to the same beach in Florida, smoked the same brand of cigarettes, built a white bench around a tree in his garden, and had worked as a deputy sheriff.

The question for researchers is: Can all these, and other similarities, be attributed to coincidence or genetic programming — or did some form of ESP link between the Jim twins influence their matching decisions and behavior?

> **Dorothy died from an accidental overdose of sleeping pills at her Brighton home just a few hours before a cable arrived to tell her that her twin had died in South Africa.**

Winston Churchill in London in May 1940

Unknown Guest (1987), Churchill went to get into his limousine but for some reason ignored the door that had been opened for him. Instead, he walked around to the far side of the car, opened that door and climbed in. Throughout the journey, Churchill remained on the side across from the one on which he normally sat. As the car sped through London a bomb suddenly exploded alongside it, lifting it on two wheels and nearly causing it to somersault. Churchill said later that it must have been his weight that kept the car down.

Changing sides

When Churchill's wife asked him why he had sat on the other side of the car that night, the prime minister said at first that he did not know. Then he told her, "Of course I know. Something said 'Stop!' before I reached the car door held open for me. It appeared to me that I was meant to open the door on the other side and get in and sit there — and that's what I did."

In 1986 English coal miner Gary Bexton had a financially beneficial ESP experience when he awoke at 5:00 A.M. one day with an overwhelming urge to fill in a soccer pool coupon. He was so convinced he was going to win that he even told his colleagues about his impending triumph. Thus Bexton was not surprised when he was informed that he had won more than £130,000 (over $200,000).

pipes did not burst in high summer.

"At this I decided on a fatuous compromise: I would leave the water turned on as he wished and take a key to our builder for him to use when the pipe burst. He too explained that water pipes never burst in the summer. I had the strength of mind to press the key into his reluctant hand, thank him and fly. The pipe did burst."

Evasive action

Sir Winston Churchill sometimes felt similar compulsions to act as a result of inner urgings. One evening during the Second World War, he was entertaining three government ministers at dinner at No. 10 Downing Street. London was being bombed at the time, but the dinner continued. Suddenly the prime minister went into the kitchen and spoke to the cook: "Put dinner on a hot plate in the dining room," he said and then told everyone in the kitchen to go quickly to the bomb shelter. He returned to his guests and continued with dinner. Within three minutes a bomb hit No. 10, destroying the kitchen, but leaving the diners unharmed.

On another occasion, recorded by researcher Brian Inglis in his book *The*

> ## Churchill returned to his guests and continued with dinner. Within three minutes a bomb hit No. 10, destroying the kitchen.

Such hunches have been responsible for making fortunes for business people too, many of whom readily admit to using "executive ESP" in their jobs. Hotel tycoon Conrad Hilton once said: "I've been accused more than once of playing hunches...I further believe most people have them, whether they follow them or not." He told of an occasion in the 1940's when he advised Duncan Harris, president of a large real estate

> ## "I've been accused more than once of playing hunches...

> # I further believe most people have them, whether they follow them or not."
> **Conrad Hilton**

> # "Another figure kept coming, $180,000....I changed my bid to the larger figure on that hunch. When they were opened the closest bid to mine was $179,800."

business, to buy Waldorf-Astoria bonds at a time when their price had tumbled to under five cents with little prospect of improvement because of wartime difficulties. Against his better judgment Harris bought the bonds, as did a few other people who backed "Connie's hunches." When hotel securities boomed later, they all made a great deal of money.

On another occasion Hilton bid for the Stevens Corporation when it came on the market. Trustees had called for signed, sealed bids, with the business being sold to the highest bidder. "No businessman likes sealed bids," Hilton commented after the sale. "My first bid, hastily made, was $165,000. Then somehow that didn't feel right to me. Another figure kept coming, $180,000. It satisfied me. It seemed fair. It felt right. I changed my bid to the larger figure on that hunch. When they were opened the closest bid to mine was $179,800. I got the Stevens Corporation by a narrow margin of $200. Eventually the assets returned me $2 million."

Wall Street investment millionaire Jesse Livermore was so confident of his hunches that he even interrupted his spring vacation in early 1906 so that he could obey a strong intuition to "sell short on Union Pacific."

There was no logical reason for such an impulse, but a few days later the San Francisco earthquake wrecked miles of the railway track, and the company's stock dropped dramatically. Livermore made a quarter of a million dollars by selling when he did.

Others who have spoken openly of their hunches are Alexander M. Poniatoff (founder and chairman of the

> # There was no logical reason for such an impulse, but a few days later the San Francisco earthquake wrecked miles of the railway track, and the company's stock dropped dramatically.

Emanuel Swedenborg

BLAZING VISION

Emanuel Swedenborg, the 18th-century Swedish scientist and mystic, was known for his remarkable psychic powers. One evening in July 1759, Swedenborg was staying with other guests at a merchant's house in Gothenburg. Suddenly Swedenborg became very upset and said that he could "see" a serious fire near his own home in Stockholm, nearly 300 miles away. Swedenborg began to relax as he "saw" the fire coming under control. Two days later, news of the fire reached Gothenburg through normal communication channels. Swedenborg's descriptions, which he had given in front of witnesses, exactly matched the actual circumstances of the fire.

Disastrous effects
At 5:13 a.m. on April 18, 1906, a huge earthquake left San Francisco completely devastated. The resultant fire burned for three days, destroying 512 blocks and 28,000 buildings in the center of town, together with miles of Union Pacific's railway track, and causing damage of approximately $500 million. This photograph shows the damaged City Hall immediately after the earthquake had hit.

POPULAR PREDICTIONS

One aspect of ESP is precognition, or knowing the future. Not suprisingly when a newsworthy disaster occurs, many people come forward to claim prior knowledge of the event. Yet most of these claims are impossible to validate because they are made after the incident. However, some tragic events do seem to have been predicted with chilling accuracy.

I N 1898 A NEW YORK AUTHOR, Morgan Robertson, had published a novel called *Futility: The Wreck of the Titan,* in which a great liner called the *Titan,* regarded as unsinkable and indestructible, collided with an iceberg and sank. Because there were not nearly enough lifeboats on board the ship, many of the passengers and crew drowned.

In the 1880's, the English journalist W. T. Stead had written a fictional story along similar lines about a huge ocean liner sinking in the mid-Atlantic. In 1892

Death at sea
An artist's impression of the sinking Titanic.

Stead wrote another story about a collision between an ocean liner and an iceberg. As a result of the research for his writing, Stead became anxious about the need for satisfactory safety precautions on board ships, and in 1910 he gave a lecture on the subject. He described what it might be like to abandon ship in icy waters, and he gave a warning concerning the need to provide enough lifeboats to accommodate all of the passengers on oceangoing vessels.

By 1910 work had started on a new ocean liner called the *Titanic,* and while it was still under construction, Stead felt a compelling urge to visit several psychics. He said these clairvoyants warned him that "travel would be dangerous in the month of April 1912" and that he would be "in the midst of a catastrophe at sea." Despite the warnings and his own unease, Stead booked a passage on the *Titanic's* maiden voyage, scheduled for April 10, 1912.

As the ship set out from Southampton, England, most people along the coast cheered. However, when the ship passed the Isle of Wight, the Marshall family was watching from the roof of their home, and suddenly Mrs. Marshall reportedly screamed that the liner was going to sink. She had a clear image of the *Titanic* going under and passengers struggling in the icy water. Mrs. Marshall shouted hysterically that something should be done to save the people, but no one listened, apart from her young daughter, Joan, who wrote about the incident as an adult.

At 11:40 P.M. on April 14, the Titanic struck an iceberg while traveling at full speed, despite having received repeated warnings that there were icebergs in

Over 2,200 passengers desperately tried to find room on the 20 available lifeboats aboard the vessel, and many of the men courageously gave up their places to women and children.

the vicinity. In a little over three hours the great liner disappeared under the water. Over 2,200 passengers desperately tried to find room on the 20 available lifeboats aboard the vessel, and many of the men courageously gave up their places to women and children. Tragically, over 1,500 people died in the freezing waters that night. Author W. T. Stead was among them.

From the ocean floor
In 1987 a French-American Titanic *expedition recovered numerous artifacts from the wreckage and the ocean floor around it. This is the ship's telegraph, which was used to send orders from the bridge to the engine room.*

Childish attitudes

Children tend to score better on ESP tests than adults. This may be because children are much less skeptical than adults. Research has shown that believers and extroverts seem to have more psychic ability than skeptics and introverts.

board of Ampex Corporation), William W. Keeler (board chairman of Phillips Petroleum), and John E. Fetzer (chairman of Fetzer Broadcasting Company and owner of the Detroit Tigers). These men were among those who spoke of their belief in ESP powers in *Psychic* magazine in December 1974.

Profit and loss

But are these exceptional individuals, or is there, then, evidence that successful business people have greater psychic powers than most other humans? John Mihalasky and E. Douglas Dean of the Newark College of Engineering in New Jersey conducted a study of corporation presidents attending business conferences. They discovered a significant statistical link between profits over a five-year period and the ability of the executives to score above chance levels in a 100-number precognition experiment.

If ESP is available so freely, why wait for hunches? Why not harness it to good effect? Stanford Research Institute scientist Harold Puthoff and his team had this thought after conducting successful laboratory ESP tests. The Stanford team decided to test their own ability to use ESP to win at gambling. In 1974 the four men drove to a gambling casino at

Lake Tahoe on the California-Nevada border. The men waited for the roulette wheel to spin a double zero, the agreed starting point. The team immediately began placing modest bets of $5 on their predetermined, ESP-inspired choices and, within a few spins, they were $100 winners.

Such an experiment is valueless in scientific terms, but it gave the team confidence to pursue their ESP research with renewed vigor.

Not that ESP is about winning fortunes. ESP might exist, if it exists at all, like most of our other faculties — to aid our self-preservation. Harold Puthoff and his wife, Adrienne, discovered this when their parapsychologist colleague, Russell Targ and his wife, Joan, joined them for dinner at their home in Palo Alto, California. Halfway through a very enjoyable evening, Joan Targ stood up and said she and Russell had to leave immediately. Everyone wanted to know why, but she could not think of a tangible reason except to

> **The team immediately began placing modest bets of $5 on their predetermined, ESP-inspired choices and, within a few spins they were $100 winners.**

Women talking

Researchers have found that women appear to have more ESP experiences than men, especially as "receivers" of signals. Although this might show a difference in psychic abilities, it could also reflect the stereotyped roles of the genders.

say that since they did not have any curtains hung, someone might look in and see the sleeping children.

Targ describes what happended next in *The Mind Race*, a book about understanding and using psychic ability, which he co-wrote with fellow researcher Keith Harary in 1985. "In fact, when we arrived home a few minutes later, we opened the front door and faintly heard someone coughing. We went into the bedroom of our 10-year-old son, Sandy, and found him quietly choking to death. He had already turned blue from lack of oxygen. Joan, a registered nurse, knew what to do. She dragged him into the bathroom, turned on the hot shower full blast, and turned the room into a large croup tent. Within a few minutes the room was filled with steam. Sandy resumed breathing and went back to sleep. We, however, were so frightened by the experience that we slept on the floor of his room."

For the Targs and thousands of others, ESP is very much a part of their everyday lives, and they are grateful for it. However, many researchers believe that ESP not only affects

the living but the dying as well. Occasionally when someone dies, particularly if the death is sudden or violent, a relative or friend reports seeing that person at that moment or within a few hours of death. The vision is usually so real that it does not occur to the viewer that they might be looking at a ghost. For example, Eldred Bowyer-Bower was shot down and killed over France during the First World War, on March 19, 1917. His half-sister, thousands of miles away in India, was caring for her baby at the time. Suddenly, she had a strong urge to turn round. She did so and to her amazement saw her brother standing in the room with her.

"I was simply delighted to see him and turned back quickly to put the baby in a safe place on the bed so that I could go on talking to my brother. I then turned again and put my hand out to him but I found he was not there." Later she discovered that Eldred had died on the same day that she had this experience. Did Eldred's sister see a spirit returning from the dead to prove that it was alive in another world, or might there be another explanation?

Telepathic dramatizations

One possibility, according to researchers, is that such apparitions are the result of telepathy between the person who is dying and the individual who sees the vision. Among the psychical experts who have argued along these lines is G. N. M. Tyrrell. In his book *Apparitions* (1953), Tyrrell suggested that hallucinatory images are like sensory images, and that the subconscious mind might pick up a telepathic thought that a friend or relative is dying. The information then finds its way into the conscious mind by being dramatized, either immediately or some hours later, in the form of a vision of the dying person.

> # The subconscious mind might pick up a telepathic thought that a friend or relative is dying. The information then finds its way into the conscious mind.

DEADLY VISIONS

A number of people claim to have seen, with precognition, the assassination of President John F. Kennedy, which took place in Dallas, on November 22, 1963. For example, in the summer of 1963, television comedian Red Skelton was dozing on a beach. He awoke to find himself writing something "automatically" on paper. Skelton was astonished to see that he had written: "President Kennedy will be killed in November."

Skelton was not known for possessing psychic abilities, unlike seer Jeane Dixon. In 1952 Dixon says that she was praying at St. Matthew's Cathedral in Washington D.C., when she suddenly had a vision of the White House, with the numbers 1-9-6-0 above it. A voice then told Dixon that a Democrat inaugurated as president in 1960 would be assassinated in office. Eleven years later, just a few weeks before the president's death in Dallas, Dixon told a friend of the Kennedys: "The president has just made a decision to go someplace in the South that will be fatal for him. You must get word to him not to make the trip."

Double tragedy

Dixon also claims to have predicted the death of Robert Kennedy. At a convention in the Ambassador Hotel, in Los Angeles, Dixon asked for questions from the floor. Someone inquired if Robert Kennedy would become president. Dixon said that he wouldn't, because of "a tragedy right here." A week later, in the very same Ambassador Hotel, Kennedy was shot.

CASEBOOK
VISIONS OF DEATH

Bentine went ice cold as the manservant explained to him that, at the last minute Walker had volunteered for a flight with a particularly inexperienced crew.

During the second world war, British comedian Michael Bentine was a young airman based at Wickenby Airfield in Lincolnshire. Before Bentine went on 48 hours leave to visit his family in London, the last person he saw was a navigator friend Flt. Lt. Walker. The flight lieutenant was known as Pop to most of his colleagues, because he was older than the rest of them. Walker had just completed his first tour of the required 30 missions, and he too was apparently about to depart on leave to visit his wife and their children.

Silent acknowledgment
Bentine returned from his leave just before midnight on a bright, moonlit night. As he reached his Nissen hut in the woods, he saw the "tall, moustachioed figure" of Pop Walker. Bentine waved at the flight lieutenant, who appeared to acknowledge him before turning off toward his own quarters. As a cloud suddenly covered the moon, Bentine crept back to his hut under cover of darkness. He undressed as quickly as possible so as not to disturb his sleeping colleagues, and within minutes he was himself sound asleep. It seemed but seconds later when he was rudely awaked by the noise of his batman (officer's personal attendant) coming in with a cup of tea and water for shaving. It was 6:30 A.M.

"Have a nice forty-eight?" the batman inquired, and then added with a touch of sadness, "Awful shame about Mr. Walker."

"What do you mean? I saw him only last night!" Bentine protested.

"You couldn't have, sir," the batman replied. "He was dead long before then."

Bentine went ice cold as the manservant explained to him that, at the last minute Walker had volunteered for a flight with a particularly inexperienced crew. The pilot became lost and the plane hit high ground and exploded. No one survived the accident.

However, Bentine remained adamant that he had indeed seen Walker the previous night. But had he witnessed the appearance of a ghost, or had unknown powers of extrasensory perception made him suddenly aware that something terrible had happened? And had this awareness manifested itself in the form of an unexplained vision?

CASEBOOK
LIFESAVING DREAM

*Following her dream,
Señora Casas
became increasingly
concerned about
Perez, so she
hurriedly walked to
the police station
to raise the alarm.*

I N 1980 IN BARCELONA, 80-year-old
Señora Isabel Casas had a terrible
dream during which she saw the face of
her neighbor, Rafael Perez, "twisted in terror,"
and heard a voice saying, "They are going to
kill us." Following her dream, Señora Casas
became increasingly concerned about Perez,
so she hurriedly walked to the police station to
raise the alarm.

Puzzling correspondence
At first, the police were inclined to dismiss her
fears. But they became curious when she told
them that Perez, the only other resident in the
apartment block, normally called to see her
every day but had not done so for 10 days.
What puzzled them, and Señora Casas, was
that Perez had written a note to her saying
that he was going away for several weeks. But
the note had not been delivered until three
days after she had last seen him. Besides, it was
unusual for him not to call in and see her in
order to tell her this news personally.

The police decided to search Perez's apartment
and the surrounding area for clues to his
whereabouts. They finally found him tied up in a utility
room on the roof of the apartment block in which he
and Señora Casas lived. Perez told the police that two
men had broken into his apartment and made him sign
28 checks so that they could withdraw his life savings
from the bank. They then forced him to write the note
to Señora Casas explaining his absence and said that
once they had all of his money, they would return to
kill him and the old lady. The police were able to set a
trap; they lay in wait for the criminals and arrested
them when they returned to carry out their gruesome
plan. Perez was convinced that Señora Casas's vivid
dream had saved both their lives.

Russian scientists have been researching telepathic powers since the 1930's, and many political leaders in eastern Europe have shown an interest in the possible military and strategic value of ESP phenomena.

In his book *Minds Without Boundaries* (1976) author Stuart Holroyd reported an incident that involved the Soviet dictator Joseph Stalin. According to Holroyd, Stalin heard in 1940 about the impressive powers of Wolf Messing, a Polish psychic. Stalin suggested that an interesting test of Messing's abilities would be to see if he could rob a bank using telepathy.

Monetary gain

The psychic selected a large bank in Moscow in which to carry out his psychic demonstration. When Messing walked into the bank, he handed a teller a blank piece of paper torn from a school notebook. Messing then put his

Polish psychic Wolf Messing

case on the counter and mentally instructed the clerk to hand over 100,000 rubles.

The clerk reportedly opened the safe and put 100,000 rubles into Messing's bag. Messing walked out of the building and showed the money to two of Stalin's assistants to prove that the robbery had been successful. Messing then went back into the bank and returned the cash to the teller. When the dumbfounded man looked at the money, the story goes, he realized what he had done and collapsed.

LOOKING FOR PROOF

"Unless there is a gigantic conspiracy involving some 30 university departments all over the world...the only conclusion the unbiased observer can come to must be that there does exist a small number of people who obtain knowledge existing either in other people's minds, or in the outer world, by means yet unknown to science."
Dr. Hans Eysenck

THE MOST REMARKABLE long-distance ESP experiment was performed in 1971, with the sender and subject nearly 240,000 miles apart. While walking on the moon during the Apollo 14 space mission, American astonaut Edgar Mitchell tried sending a series of numbers to a psychic on earth. The results were said to have been above those predicted by chance, but a single experiment of this kind is not proof of ESP. Science requires experiments that can be repeated over and over again. And for more than a century, parapsychologists have been trying to create repeatable tests, with varying degrees of success.

For more than a century, parapsychologists have been trying to create repeatable tests, with varying degrees of success.

One of the first scientists to conduct ESP experiments was Sir William Barrett, professor of physics at the Royal College of Science in Dublin. He made a 13-year study of hypnosis, during which he became convinced that he had observed psychic phenomena. Barrett presented his findings to the anthropological department of the British Association for the Advancement of Science in 1876.

Secret image

Most of the early work on ESP research involved individuals with extraordinary talents, such as Polish engineer Stephan Ossowiecki, who could apparently "see" hidden objects. In one test with Ossowiecki, an English psychical researcher, Dr. Eric Dingwall, drew a flag with a bottle in the upper left-hand corner of a piece of paper. Underneath the drawing he wrote the date: "Aug 23, 1923."

This drawing was placed in three sealed envelopes, one inside the other, and sent to another eminent investigator, Baron Albert von Schrenck-Notzing, a

ZENER CARDS

During the 1930's Dr. Karl E. Zener at the Duke University parapsychology laboratory came up with the idea for a set of cards for use in ESP tests. Each card shows one of five different symbols: a circle, a square, a star, a cross and wavy lines. A deck consists of five cards showing each symbol, a total of 25 cards in all. These cards became known as Zener cards and were used in laboratory experiments until the 1960's when more technologically advanced equipment became available.

A typical experiment using Zener cards involved a subject trying to identify each card as it is drawn. By the laws of chance, someone might expect to be correct on five cards out of a deck of 25. If a subject scores above an average of five over a long series of runs, it is possible to speculate that some other, unknown factor may be at work. On a series of 100 or more runs, even an average of six or seven hits is significant. One young woman tested by Prof. Bernard Riess at Hunter College in New York City reportedly scored an amazing 18 hits per run.

Dr. Eric Dingwall

German pathologist, who was attending an international conference on psychical research in Warsaw. Neither the baron nor two other researchers who conducted the experiment knew what Dingwall had placed in the sealed envelopes. But when Ossowiecki held the envelope, he reportedly was able to tell that it did not contain a written message, and he said that there were several envelopes, something green (cardboard) and a little bottle. He then drew an almost identical version of the target image, with the figures "1923" below, and said that something else was written before this, but that he could not read it. Such demonstrations have led many researchers to come to accept the reality of clairvoyance.

Yet if some individuals perform so well, it is at least theoretically possible that other people may also have psychic powers. Among the early investigators who tried mass experiments to detect possible ESP abilities was researcher René Warcollier. He conducted a series of tests in the 1920's, attempting to transmit feelings and visual images by telepathy. Some of Warcollier's experiments were carried out in his native France and others between France and the United States. In fact, instead of having just one sender and one receiver, he used groups of people concentrating on the same image or emotion. Many sensations were supposedly transmitted successfully, and the results over long distances were reportedly impressive. But there was little evidence to suggest that ESP worked more effectively with a group than with individuals.

Experimental structure

Meanwhile, a well-known British psychologist, William McDougall, had been appointed to the chair of psychology at Harvard University in 1920, where he began a program of extensive psychic research. McDougall had become interested in the paranormal while a student at Cambridge University in England, and by the time he moved to Harvard he was president of Britain's Society for Psychical Research. Once in the U.S. he soon found funds to start experimental telepathy work. Among the psychologists who carried out these tests was Gardner Murphy, who had worked with René Warcollier in the France-U.S.A. experiments. By 1926 the Harvard researchers were joined by a young Chicago botanist, Joseph Banks Rhine. He joined the psychology department as a research assistant and went to Duke University with McDougall when he moved there a year later.

Within eight years, Rhine had coined the phrase "extrasensory perception" (ESP) and made it a household word, with the publication of his controversial book of the same title. In his book he claimed that experiments at Duke University had produced overwhelming proof of the

> # He then drew an almost identical version of the target image, with the figures "1923" below.

▶ PAGE 81

THE GANZFELD STATE

*Ganzfeld **is a German word meaning "uniform field,"** **and in 1971 parapsychologist Charles Honorton** **developed the Ganzfeld state — an environment in which** **the brain is deprived of virtually all sensory input.** **Honorton and other paranormal researchers believe** **that if all sensory stimulus is removed, the brain's** **attention focuses on internal mental events and becomes** **more sensitive to ESP.***

A subject in the Ganzfeld state

*D*URING AN EXPERIMENT that took place in 1981, in Cambridge, England, young computer expert Hugh Ashton made himself comfortable on a mattress, placed halved table tennis balls and cotton wool over his eyes and then put on earphones that emitted white noise. Unable to see or hear anything that would distract him — the Ganzfeld state — he was ready to begin an ESP test.

Soon Ashton began describing impressions and shapes that came into his mind, trying to capture the essence of a target picture that a sender was concentrating on in another room. That picture had been selected at random from four possible targets.

Gradually, as Ashton spoke of different images, a picture began to form. His words were recorded by the experimenter, Dr. Carl Sargent of Cambridge University, who was unaware, at that stage, of the picture that had been selected.

"Keep thinking of firemen and fire station," Ashton said. "Firemen definitely seen, black and white. People but not faces. I think one man at bottom in foreground: facing...young face, as if photographer says, 'Oi' and only he turned round."

At the end of the session, all four potential target pictures were brought into the laboratory and Ashton was asked to identify the one he thought the agent had been trying to send telepathically. He had no difficulty in doing so because one was a photograph, exactly as he had described, of firemen playing hoses on a training building. Their backs are to the camera, but just one has turned and is looking straight at the photographer. Ashton was one of Dr. Sargent's top-scoring subjects, but others were also uncannily accurate

when they took part in ESP tests. In fact, the images formed in the mind of one subject were so positive and recognizable that he was able to identify the target picture by name before the session ended. It was William Blake's painting "The Ancient of Days."

Measuring success

These were two of the outstanding successes that Sargent recorded during his extensive tests. The results convinced him that sensory deprivation was an excellent way of enhancing ESP sensitivity and, on average, he believed that he obtained results that were 17 percent above chance. Sargent may be the best known of the Ganzfeld experimenters, but he was not the first. That honor goes to Charles Honorton and Sharon Harper in the United States, who used this technique to explore ESP in the early 1970's, employing 30 subjects. The subjects scored 13 direct hits, and the chances of that happening are estimated at 58 to 1.

Although some parapsychologists believe that the use of the Ganzfeld state has, at last, given them the means of producing a repeatable psychic experiment, others are not convinced. Among them is British parapsychologist Dr. Susan Blackmore, who studied the Cambridge work and took part in a Ganzfeld session with Sargent's team. Dr. Blackmore maintained that there were weaknesses in the laboratory's controls. Other critics have suggested that it was possible for subjects to manipulate the randomizing cards.

These arguments concerning Sargent's work provoked a bitter dispute. Some time later Sargent wrote: "I don't care whether people think I'm a fraud or not, but I object very strongly to anyone believing that I might be a stupid one."

> **He was able to identify the target picture by name.... It was William Blake's "The Ancient of Days."**

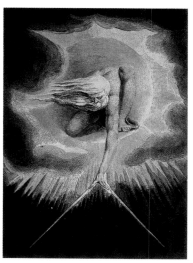

William Blake's painting "The Ancient of Days"

79

FAKING IT

There are various methods of obtaining information by normal means during ESP tests, even when elaborate precautions have been taken to guard against cheating. This is why many parapsychologists are now seeking the help of magicians in developing controls for their experiments.

Sir Oliver Lodge

W HEN THE FAMOUS BRITISH physicist Sir Oliver Lodge carried out telepathy tests with two girls who claimed to be able to read each other's minds, he was convinced that they had special powers, and said as much in his book, *The Survival of Man* (1909). But the experiment was flawed because he allowed the girls to hold hands while they were trying to communicate the images of playing cards, and this gave them an opportunity make surreptitious use of a code. If that was not the case, then why did the girls' scores drop virtually to chance levels when they were not allowed to touch hands?

A similar fraudulent technique was used by the Creery Sisters, daughters of an English clergyman, to hoodwink a committee on thought reading that was set up in the early 1880's in England by the Society for Psychical Research. Among those who were taken in by the girls'

Experimental control
In 1983 a Chinese child named Xiong Jie impressed researchers when she produced the images on the left, having "read" the concealed target drawings shown on the right. Critics now claim that controls during such experiments were not strict enough.

> ## "Even if you can't explain something, that doesn't make it supernatural."

demonstrations were leading scientists and psychical researchers of the day.

In the 1930's general interest in ESP was so great that sets of the Duke University Zener cards were made available to the public in the form of "test your ESP" kits. It was soon pointed out by a number of researchers, however, that under certain strong lighting conditions, it was possible to see the pictures on the cards through their backs. Did this straightforward explanation account for successful ESP results?

Such simple card-guessing experiments were the backbone of much early ESP research — and are still conducted today. But in some of these tests the subject was allowed to handle the cards, face down, as he or she guessed what was on the reverse. It is quite feasible that, over a series of tests, the subject might learn to recognize certain cards by their appearance or feel — or even mark them with a fingernail scratch — so that a

hit might be scored each time a particular card came up. This may sound far-fetched but such methods are the stock-in-trade of many a good magician, and it was noted that a number of high-scoring subjects were less successful when they were not allowed to see or touch the cards.

Searching for clues
Research has been carried out with children in China in which they described pictures and words sealed in containers. And in the United States, tests have also been carried out with people who are blind. But even in such cases there is always the chance that either tactile or auditory clues might be picked up by the subjects.

To show people how easy it is to be fooled into believing they have witnessed paranormal phenomena, Scot Morris, who holds a Ph.D. in clinical psychology, used to hold "special" lab sessions while teaching at Southern Illinois University. He would introduce to the students an ESP expert who would give a demonstration. He first "received" a number between one and 20, a number the class had agreed upon while he was out of the room. He then spoke of having developed a strong ESP bond with a friend and said he would "send" a picture of a particular playing card selected from a pack. Three students went to a phone to call the person in question and returned with the amazing news that he had got it right. Finally, the demonstrator "read" and answered questions, written by six students and sealed in envelopes, simply by holding them to his forehead.

Although about 80 percent of the class believed they had seen a demonstration of genuine ESP, they had in fact merely witnessed simple parlor tricks. Yet Morris would not explain how the deceptions were achieved. He wanted to leave his students with the feeling that "even if you can't explain something, that doesn't necessarily make it supernatural."

existence of ESP. According to Rhine, it was not until his third set of experiments that he began to encounter positive results. Using Zener cards, Rhine asked 24 subjects to guess which symbol was on a card that was face down. Out of 800 guesses, the subjects managed 207 correct answers. Since there was a choice of five symbols, Rhine calculated that the results would have been about 160 hits if only chance were involved. The chances of achieving this sort of success rate were calculated at more than a million to one against.

Impromptu testing

During the early 1930's, Rhine and his team began refining their experiments and controlling them more stringently. They also decided to concentrate on particularly high-scoring subjects, such as psychology students Adam J. Linzmayer and Charles E. Stuart. Linzmayer achieved the best results

Charles E. Stuart

when distracted while making his guesses; so Rhine sometimes took him out for a drive, stopping occasionally for impromptu ESP tests. On one occasion, the young student was correct on all 15 cards. Such uncontrolled experiments may have convinced Rhine but, as a scientist, he knew that they would have little value in research circles. However, Linzmayer continued to produce impressive scores in the Duke lab.

Faced with Rhine's claims, skeptics looked for weaknesses in his experimental procedures and errors in his statistical analysis. One critic was

Bernard Riess, a psychologist, who apparently questioned Rhine so aggressively after a lecture that the Duke University researcher protested that he was being called a liar. But rather than be defensive, Rhine encouraged Riess to conduct his own ESP experiments, using all the controls he believed were required. Urged by his own students to accept the challenge, Riess carried out a series of card-guessing experiments with a young woman who claimed to be psychic. In 74 runs of 25 cards (1,850 guesses) she produced an astonishing average of 18 hits out of 25 attempts.

In 1938, speaking at an ESP symposium organized by the American Psychological Association, Riess declared that no criticism could be made of the methods used in his experiments. He explained that he had the deck of cards on his desk, shuffled them and turned them over, one by one, at the stated time, making a record of

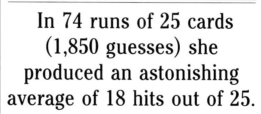

In 74 runs of 25 cards (1,850 guesses) she produced an astonishing average of 18 hits out of 25.

each card as he did so. Sometimes it was a week before he checked the totals. "The only error that may have crept in," he added, "is a possibility of deception. The only person who could have done the deceiving was myself since the subject at no time knew how well she was doing nor had any idea of the cards which were being turned by myself."

Statistical approval

The suggestion that there was something wrong with Rhine's statistics was also scotched, in 1937, by the American Institute of Mathematical Statistics. It carried out an investigation of the Duke University results and validated the statistical methods used to evaluate Rhine's ESP tests.

Adam J. Linzmayer

> "The only error that may have crept in, is a possibility of deception. The only person who could have done the deceiving was myself since the subject at no time knew how well she was doing nor had any idea of the cards which were being turned by myself."
> **Bernard Riess**

REMOTE VIEWING

In their 1985 publication **The Mind Race,** *researchers Russell Targ and Keith Harary described many remarkable experiments in which subjects tried to describe target locations miles away. One experiment, however, involving freelance photographer Hella Hammid, proved to be quite remarkable.*

Hella Hammid

IN 1978 HELLA HAMMID sat down with parapsychologist Russell Targ in a comfortable, windowless room, on the third floor of the radio physics building at the Stanford Research Institute (SRI) in Palo Alto, California. She had recently taken part in six remote viewing experiments with Targ, with a 50 percent success rate, and she was eager to try a seventh test. So she prepared herself to "send" her mind in search of a specific target.

Two members of Targ's experimental team went to the second floor of the building, where they used a device known as an electronic random-number generator to produce a code that they passed to Targ's secretary. She opened her safe and took out a metal box containing 60 envelopes, each holding different instructions that would determine the destination to be used in the experiment. She then selected the envelope that carried the matching code. Only when the two team members were in their car did they open the envelope to discover the target. The card read: "AIRPORT TOWER — Cross Bayshore Freeway on Embarcadero Road. On your left will be the Palo Alto Airport. Follow the airport road to its end, which will take you to the tower. Notice the square concrete base, and pentagonal glass top. Walk around the tower, look up at it. Also notice the aircraft nearby, and the surrounding trees."

Targ referred to the helpers as "beacons," for their role was not to try sending images telepathically but simply to be present at the site. The beacons provided a human link to help the subject tune in to the place that had been selected.

A full record of Hella's impressions was made. The following dialogue is edited from the conversation between the interviewer, Russell Targ (RT), and the subject, Hella Hammid (HH):

HH: It looks like a large cabbage shape, with inter-connected petals, around the base of this towerlike building. The tower has a thing on top.

RT: Can you tell me anything about the shape of the tower?

HH: It seems to be quite square, with four corners,

and has a sort of enlarged tip at the top.

RT: Will you be able to draw that for me later?

HH: I have begun to draw that right here. It is as if the tower was standing in a slight depression, with either mounds of earth piled up around it or with these leaflike protrusions — or as if it grew organically out the center of a plant. It doesn't seem like a huge tower.

RT: You said that it is enlarged at the top....

HH: Slightly, yes. There seems to be an extra piece around it, with some kind of cross grid. I sense that it is something mechanical that needs to be visible from the sky, and that's directional. Definitely a kind of marker....

RT: What are our friends doing?

HH: I see them not too close to the tower. I have the feeling that they can't get too close. It is not an inhabited building. It is not something that you live in. I get more the feeling that it is some technical installation. Like a weather station, or an airport tower, or a radar installation or radio.... No, it's not radio. It's not that high, and it's not metal. It's a mixture of stone and metal.

> **Targ referred to the helpers as "beacons," for their role was not to try sending images telepathically but simply to be present at the site.**

Right on target

Targ commented that it was remarkable for Hella to identify the target as possibly an airport tower. He said that this particular location had not been selected in previous tests and that Hella had never seen it.

Targ added that this was also an excellent example of what is right and wrong with remote viewing. Hella was at times very specific and accurate in her descriptions. At other times she was unable to clarify vague impressions about what was at the base of the tower. She spoke of "winglike projections." Her images of trees and airplanes became somewhat confused. Nonetheless, this experiment was judged to be quite exceptional — and a hit.

The one explanation that is "simplest and most in accord with everyday experience," he argued, was fraud by the experimenters themselves.

Yet there was another possible, non-paranormal, explanation for the remarkable results, one that had to be voiced. In 1955 *Science*, the official journal of the American Association for the Advancement of Science, published an article by medical researcher G. R. Price. The one explanation that is "simplest and most in accord with everyday experience," he argued, was fraud by the experimenters themselves. Dr. Rhine and Dr. S. G. Soal, a well-known British parapsychologist, of Queen Mary College, London University, were the main targets of this suggestion.

About turn

Although some people believed that Price had successfully "exposed" Dr. Rhine, who was by this time director of the Duke parapsychology laboratory, Rhine took it calmly and entered into a lengthy correspondence with Price, answering in depth all the questions

Basil Shackleton

raised about procedures and controls. These exchanges resulted, 17 years later, in another *Science* article by Price, entitled "Apology to Rhine and Soal."

In fact, Price's initial suggestion of fraud was correct with regard to Soal. Britain's best-known psychical researcher was one of a number of investigators who tried unsuccessfully to repeat Rhine's ESP results. For five years from 1934, following the publication of Rhine's book, Soal carried out tests with 160 people in an attempt to record evidence for telepathy or clairvoyance. He found none in the 128,350 guesses recorded, and as well as being skeptical, Soal was also very critical of Rhine's experimental controls.

Displacement effect

Soal claimed later that he was advised in 1939 to re-examine his earlier ESP results by Cambridge psychical researcher Whately Carington. While carrying out his own experiments into telepathy, Carington had found that some subjects seemed to be guessing — not the card that was the target but the one before or after. Soal said he found the same phenomenon in two of the people he tested, Mrs. G. Stewart and Basil Shackleton. Encouraged by this finding, he started a new investigation in 1941, in collaboration with Mrs. K. M. Goldney, a Society for Psychical Research council member.

Shackleton was the subject of 40 tests held between 1941 and 1943, using cards depicting animals instead of Zener cards. A list of random numbers was used in each experiment to select the order in which the cards had to be guessed to be correct. The results of these and other tests with different subjects were impressive and appeared to confirm that a displacement effect, either one or two cards ahead, was occurring with certain people. Soal appeared to have come up with outstanding evidence for ESP, and his experiments convinced many experts of its existence. Cambridge philosopher R. H. Thouless went as far as to say: "The reality of the phenomena [of ESP] must be regarded as proved as certainly as anything in scientific research can be proved."

But not everyone was satisfied that Soal had been careful enough. In fact,

Dr. S. G. Soal

> "The reality of the phenomena [of ESP] must be regarded as proved as certainly as anything in scientific research can be proved."
> **R. H. Thouless**

Dr. Leonid Vasiliev

UNDISCOVERED ENERGY

Dr. Leonid Vasiliev was head of a special parapsychology laboratory at Leningrad University, where he ran hundreds of experiments into ESP. Vasiliev revealed that Russian scientists have been researching telepathy since the 1930's, under top secret orders from the government.

Priceless energy

In 1960, Vasiliev told a group of Soviet scientists that the American navy was trying to discover whether telepathy would work on atomic submarines. Vasiliev said: "The discovery of the energy underlying ESP will be equivalent to the discovery of atomic energy." Vasiliev believed that there is a physical basis for ESP ability, and he thought it operates through some kind of energy in the brain which had yet to be discovered.

> **Not surprisingly, the failure of many scientists to replicate the results of others prompted researchers to look for other ways of detecting and demonstrating ESP.**

one of the subjects in his experiments, a Mrs. Gretl Albert, claimed to have peeped through a hole in a screen that separated her from Soal during the tests. She said she saw Soal altering the figure 1 to a 4 or a 5 on a number of occasions. When psychic researcher R. G. Medhurst looked into this allegation, he found that there was an excess of hits on numbers 4 and 5. This led him and other researchers to analyze the Soal work in more detail, and they too came up with some very suspicious anomalies in the figures, suggesting that they had been tampered with.

The final nail in the coffin of this once highly regarded ESP investigator was provided by fellow researcher Betty Markwick, who carried out a computer study of the random numbers used by Soal. The numbers were taken by Soal from Chambers's logarithmic tables and Tippett's random number tables, which was standard practice. But Soal had not explained how they were used.

Fraud by numbers

In 1978 Miss Markwick showed that Soal's lists did not match the standard published ones; instead, extra digits had been inserted in the list and these almost invariably produced hits. When the extra numbers were removed, the scores were only at chance levels. Most researchers now accept Miss Markwick's damning conclusion that "all the

> **Some researchers have tried to "humanize" ESP research and move it out of the laboratory.**

experimental series in card-guessing carried out by Dr. Soal must, as the evidence stands, be discredited."

What might have been an instance of ESP could have been responsible for Betty Markwick's discovery of fraud in the case of Dr. Soal's research procedures. Miss Markwick has revealed that the initial motivation for her investigation was an intense dream in which psychic researcher R. G. Medhurst, who had by then died, appeared in the role of tutor, explaining a mathematical graphic problem that he wished her to work on. Five days later Markwick received the Society for Psychical Research's journal and found, to her astonishment, a posthumously published paper by Medhurst, the subject of which was curiously linked to her dream. This further convinced her to investigate Dr. Soal's methods. "It was difficult to resist the feeling, that an element of ESP might...be involved, impelling me to follow up certain ideas suggested by the dream," she wrote.

There has never been any serious suggestion that Dr. Rhine, who died in 1980, tampered with his results to make them appear to provide evidence for ESP. But not surprisingly, the failure of many scientists to replicate the results of others prompted researchers to look for other ways of detecting and demonstrating ESP. Thus challenged, researchers came up with automatic randomizing techniques, the first of which, called VERITAC, was used in 1963 at the United States Air Force Laboratories. This experiment failed to find any evidence of ESP. Six years later, however, Dr. Helmut Schmidt published details of research carried out at the Boeing Research Laboratories in Seattle, using a random number generator, "powered" by decaying radioactive material. Dr. Schmidt claimed that he had found evidence for ESP in 63,066 trials with three subjects, which produced odds of 500 million to 1.

But some researchers have tried to "humanize" ESP research and move it out of the laboratory. The Russians, in particular, claim some very impressive results in experiments that took place in 1966, involving Yuri Kamensky, a biophysicist, and Karl Nikolaiev, an actor and journalist. In supervised tests in which one of the subjects was in Siberia and the other in Moscow, Nikolaiev identified six objects and 12 out of 20 ESP cards that Kamensky had been shown. By attaching Nikolaiev to an electroencephalograph (EEG), researchers reportedly found that his brain waves changed the moment Kamensky began transmitting images. Scientists also detected a strong reaction in Nikolaiev when they asked Kamensky to imagine that he was fighting the biophysicist.

This led experimenters to devise an ingenious way of communicating a message that would remain a secret to both the human transmitter and the

Messages from Siberia
Under the watchful eye of a research assistant, Karl Nikolaiev concentrates on receiving long-distance telepathic communications from Yuri Kamensky.

> # "In so far as it is humanly possible to prove anything, the Schmidt experiments provide us with the final proof of both ESP and PK."

receiver. Kamensky was told to conduct mental bouts of fighting with his partner. A 45-second transmission was recorded as a Morse code dash while a 15-second bout was a dot. In this way, the subjects reportedly conveyed the Russian word *mig* (meaning "instant") in telepathic Morse code over a distance of 2,000 miles. Dr. Douglas Dean at the Newark College of Engineering in New Jersey conducted a similar experiment in the late 1960's in which a plethysmograph was used to measure changes in blood volume. He used a negative or positive response to represent a dot or dash. He apparently succeeded in sending a message between New York and Florida.

Interpreting the evidence

Thus, with so much research completed, can it be said that the existence of ESP has been proven? British researcher John Randall says: "Insofar as it is humanly possible to prove anything, the Schmidt experiments provide us with the final proof of both ESP and PK." And eminent psychologist Dr. Hans Eysenck believes that: "Unless there is a gigantic conspiracy involving some 30 university departments all over the world, and several hundred highly respected scientists in various fields, the only conclusion the unbiased observer can come to must be that there does exist a small number of people who obtain knowledge existing either in other people's minds, or in the outer world, by means yet unknown to science."

Skeptics, such as Prof. C. E. M. Hansel from the University College of Swansea, University of Wales, disagree. Prof. Hansel insists "A great deal of time, effort and money has been expended over a period of more than a hundred years, but an acceptable demonstration of the existence of extra-sensory perception or psychokinesis has not been provided."

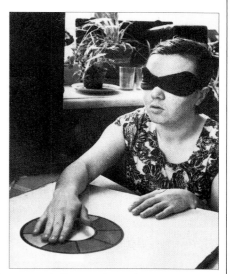

Sense of touch
Rosa Kuleshova tries to identify colors by touch.

A FEEL FOR COLOR

In 1962 a young Russian woman named Rosa Kuleshova went to her doctor and announced that she could distinguish colors with her fingertips. The doctor was reportedly impressed by her claim and arranged for her to be tested at the Biophysics Institute of the Soviet Academy of Sciences.

Skin vision

Scientists at the institute, among them Prof. Abram Novomeysky, judged that Kuleshova's skin was so sensitive that she could really "see" through her fingers. Prof. Novomeysky supposedly went on to establish that this "skin vision" is something that many people could develop. He carried out further tests and apparently found that one in six subjects could learn to distinguish two colors by touch within half an hour. Amazingly, subjects even reported a specific "feel" to different colors; for example, people seemed to agree that yellow was slippery, while orange was rough.

Subjects also said that colors appeared to have different heights. Red seemed the highest, while blue was the lowest. Prof. Novomeysky has suggested that skin sight is really an interaction between the electromagnetic fields coming from both the color and the subject's body.

TEST YOUR OWN ESP

Several methods of testing ESP have not changed since the 1930's. They are simple enough to be tried at home as well as in the laboratory. The most important rule to remember is that there is nothing to be gained from tampering with your results.

DECK OF CARDS

In any deck of playing cards, half are red and half are black. The aim of this particular test is to predict which cards are red and which are black. If you try this 100 times, the odds are that you will be correct 40 to 60 times by chance alone; so if you are accurate in more than 60 of the trials, it may be that you have shown psychic skill.

Try guessing the cards in groups. Place 10 cards face down and look at the back of each card in turn. If you think it is red, put it to the right. If you judge it to be black, put it to the left. After you have used the 10 cards, turn each pile over and count your successes. Put the cards back in the deck, reshuffle and try again.

Elimination process

A group of people can attempt to detect their extrasensory powers by playing a game that is rather like a spelling bee. Participants stand in a line facing the tester, who shuffles a deck of cards and selects one. The first person in the line is asked to say if the card is red or black. If the player is correct, he or she stays standing. If the player is wrong, he or she sits down. The tester continues to ask each player in turn to guess the color of a card, putting each card back in the deck and shuffling after every go. The cards must be returned to the deck so that there is always a 50-50 chance of a correct guess. The last person standing is the winner and may be tested further on an individual basis.

A variation on this test is for players to try and guess the suit of a card rather than the color. In this instance there is a four-in-one chance of being correct; so by chance alone the group as a whole should be correct 25 percent of the time. It is worth keeping a written record of your results to see if the overall group average is higher than chance.

VISUALIZING IMAGES

In 1930 the writer Upton Sinclair and his wife, Mary, published a book about their telepathic experiences called *Mental Radio*. In the book Mary Sinclair recorded experiments for those hoping to test their own ESP. For example, Mary Sinclair gives the following advice on how to transmit a single image:

"Relax the body as completely as possible.... Visualize a rose, or a violet — some pleasant, familiar thing which does not arouse emotional memory trains....Keep attention steady, just seeing the color or shape of the flower and nothing else. Do not think about the flower. Just look at it."

She also suggests an experiment in which you try to visualize images that have been drawn on paper:

"Ask someone to draw a half-dozen simple designs for you on cards or slips of paper, folding them so that you cannot see the contents. Each paper should be folded separately, so that it can be handled one at a time....My experience is that fragments of forms appear first. For example, a curved line, or a straight one, or two lines of a triangle. But sometimes they are so vague that one gets only a notion of how they look before they vanish."

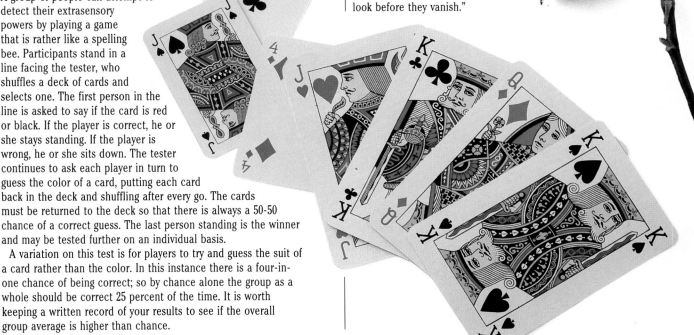

THE GANZFELD STATE

To create a Ganzfeld environment, you have to put a subject into a state of almost total sensory deprivation, in the hope that when the brain is no longer processing information affecting the five senses, the subject may have a better chance of detecting ESP.

The equipment needed to put someone into the state is relatively simple. Cut a pair of table tennis balls in half, smooth down the edges on the halves without the manufacturer's name, and then carefully place a half ball over each of the subject's eyes. Add cotton wool around the edges of the ball to block light from showing through and tape gently in place. Put a lamp with a red/orange bulb near the subject so that all that he or she can see is a soft red glow through the table tennis balls.

Place headphones over the subject's ears. The sound provided should be a hissing sound rather like a far-off waterfall, a sound known technically as white noise. One way to generate this sound is to use the steady hiss found between radio stations.

The subject lies down in this relaxed state for up to an hour. The experience should be a pleasant one, and subjects often report feelings of floating and deep relaxation. After about 10 minutes in the Ganzfeld state, the subject may well have insights or impressions to record — some people see powerful visual images or hear imaginary voices and music — so it is useful to have a tape recorder at the ready.

The next step

The experiment may be taken further by having the "carer" try to send a mental picture to the person in the Ganzfeld state. The carer should select four pictures and put them in separate envelopes. Once the subject is in the Ganzfeld state, the carer shuffles the envelopes, choses one and tries to transmit the image to the subject by concentrating on it for up to half an hour. When the subject comes out of the Ganzfeld state, he or she is shown the four different pictures and tries to identify the one that was transmitted.

TELEPATHY TRIAL

For this test involving two people, one experimenter sits behind another, with both facing in the same direction. The person at the back is the sender, and he or she looks at playing cards, one at a time, and tries to send messages to the receiver in front by thinking red or black as each card is revealed. The person in front says out loud what he or she thinks is the color of the card.

If the receiver guesses red, the sender should put the card in a pile to the right. If the receiver guesses black, the sender should put the card to the left. It is best to work on batches of 10 cards at a time, adding up and recording a score at the end of each batch.

A receiver guessing correctly more than 60 percent of the time may be showing telepathic skill, and should attempt further tests in order to clarify the results.

CHAPTER FOUR

The Divining Experience

Is it possible to use psychic powers to locate minerals, or water, or even to help solve crimes? The dowsers and diviners who claim these talents are certainly taken seriously by the oil companies that employ them and the law enforcement agencies that consult them.

Peter Harmon is a water diviner and well driller who has operated out of Portland, Maine, for over 35 years. One day he was telephoned by a prospective client in Oklahoma. Suddenly Harmon had a "vision" of the man's property even though he had never set eyes on it. He told his client: "Out in your back field you have a big doghouse. Not far from its northwest corner there is a Coca-Cola bottle lying on the ground. Your best bet to strike a

Aymar identifies a thief

UNEXPECTED FIND
Jacques Aymar lived in southern France in the late 17th century. His home town of Dauphine was known for its diviners; so perhaps it was no surprise when Aymar found that he had dowsing skills. According to one story, while dowsing for water, he dug at one particular spot indicated by his dowsing rod and found rather more than he expected — a woman's severed head. Once the woman had been identified, the story goes, Aymar visited her home and his divining rod pointed straight to her husband, identifying him as her killer. Aymar became famous for finding criminals by using his dowsing skills. He said he felt violent agitations and felt faint when pursuing murderers.

Murderous trail
In another story, Aymar was asked to find the murderer of a wine merchant and his wife. He was sure that he would be able to point to the places where the murderer had stayed while making his escape. Aymar's divining rod led him along the banks of the river Rhone. Eventually, the trail reportedly led to a prison 150 miles south of Lyon, where the rod pointed to a man recently arrested for theft. When accused of murder, the man confessed.

water well is going to be close to that bottle. Will you please go outside and check to see if it's there?"

The mystified client went outside and found the bottle as described. "How did you know about the doghouse and the bottle?" he asked Harmon when he returned to the phone. "Well," said Harmon, "it's difficult to explain, but I can see them, because I'm kinda there."

The strange abilities of diviner Peter Harmon were among several cases to come under scrutiny at the Frontiers of Physics Conference held at Reykjavik, Iceland, in 1977. At the conference controversial physicists Harold Puthoff and Russell Targ, from the Stanford Research Institute in Menlo Park, California, described various psychics they had studied. Puthoff and Targ's experiments concentrated

> ## "Well,... it's difficult to explain, but I can see them, because I'm kinda there."

on a form of dowsing known as remote viewing and were described in their book *Mind Reach*, published in 1977. For most of their experiments the two physicists selected subjects who had the ability to describe places they had never seen by visualizing them from a considerable distance.

Seeing across space
According to Puthoff and Targ, remote viewer Ingo Swann drew an accurate map of the tiny island of Kerguelen (in the southern Indian Ocean) after being given only its map coordinates. Swann was also shown the position of the planet Mercury on a celestial chart. Although claiming no knowledge of astronomy, Swann reportedly described the planet as having a thin atmosphere, a weak magnetic field, and a cometlike tail of helium. The description was contrary to scientific thought at the time

but was later shown to be accurate by information gathered by the space probe *Mariner 10* in 1974.

A second subject who worked with Puthoff and Targ at the Stanford Research Institute was a blind man. He held an item belonging to a person who was waiting at an unknown target location. Targ explained: "This man functioned as a blind person and described things in non-visual terms. He described the target location as 'hot and crowded and the sort of place you'd like to get out of once you're in it.' The mystery location was a police station."

Some of the subjects in the Puthoff and Targ experiments were totally inexperienced and even skeptical before they tried dowsing and found that they could do it. The ancient art of intuitively

Space encounter
The Mariner space probe provided much new information about the planet Mercury, some of which seemed to confirm claims by psychic Ingo Swann.

locating water or minerals underground, known as dowsing or divining, has always been something of an enigma. Dowsers traditionally hold a forked branch, known as a dowsing rod, in front of them and walk slowly across the area they are searching. When the twig moves, it is an indication that water or minerals lie beneath the earth at that spot. Many experts feel that divining works, but as yet no scientist has been able to show exactly how it does so.

In ancient times the skill was linked to witchcraft and the supernatural. Water diviners and dowsers from the southwestern counties of England referred to their dowsing powers as "water witching."

DOWSING IN VIETNAM

Marines used dowsing with considerable success in Vietnam. Despite their simplicity and low cost, military authorities have resisted giving the techniques official sanction.

Louis J. Matacia

*L*OUIS J. MATACIA is a Virginia land surveyor and a professional dowser. Using his dowsing powers, he has located oil reserves and buried treasure, underground wells and lost pipes. One of his most unusual assignments was to attempt to teach dowsing to U.S. marines for use in combat during the Vietnam War.

In November 1966 Matacia saw a film in which the U.S. secretary of defense appealed for new ideas to help solve military problems. Matacia was intrigued when he saw marines trying to find the openings to enemy tunnels in the Vietnamese jungle. He was able to locate underground utilities with a pair of divining rods made from coat hangers, and he wondered if the marines would be able to use the same technique to find enemy tunnels.

Skeptics and believers

In early 1967 Matacia volunteered to demonstrate his dowsing methods at the Marines' Development and Educational Center in Quantico, Virginia. Watched by a group of skeptical officers at Quantico, Matacia held a pair of L-shaped metal rods in his hands and walked across a large basement area under water pipes in the ceiling. As he walked under the pipes the rods swung outward and aligned with them. Matacia told the marines that the rods could be used to tell which pipes held running water as well as to find pipes under the ground. While some officers openly expressed their disbelief, others wanted to learn more.

A further test of Matacia's skills was made on a mock-up of a typical southeast Asian village located on the Quantico base. This village included such features as huts, paddy fields, bridges, and trails. The village also incorporated the kind of booby traps used by the Vietcong guerrillas, as well as tunnels, stores, secret rooms, and hiding places. The marines were curious to see if Matacia would find these underground spaces.

Matacia walked around the village with his metal diving rods held in front of him. He located a tunnel and accurately stated that it sloped downward from one house to another. Matacia continued to pass through the village, finding more tunnels, as well as underground pipes and wires. In less than half an hour, he had pinpointed most of the underground system. Under Matacia's guidance some marines tried to locate

tunnels using dowsing techniques. One young captain was amazed as his divining rods spread apart while he stood over an underground store. Matacia was encouraged by the success of the exercise and wrote confidently to a major in the Marine Corps: "I know it will work. It is inherently simple and the equipment costs almost nothing." He wrote to other officials as well, but all the responses were negative. Officially, Matacia's idea was rejected — but according to an article in *The Observer,* a newspaper for U.S. forces in Saigon (March 13, 1967), marines were using dowsing methods successfully — and unofficially.

Artist's impression of map dowsing in Vietnam

On May 12, 1968, military personnel gathered in Camp Lejeune, North Carolina, to observe a demonstration by six professional dowsers, including Louis Matacia, who had volunteered to offer training. Once again marine volunteers were taught how to locate concealed military targets in a combat zone. The dowsers also explained how to find a safe route through jungle areas without a compass, simply by using a dowsing device cut from the undergrowth, and how to pinpoint troop concentrations and airfields by swinging a pendulum over a map.

Official reluctance

Despite all the interest and success, military authorities resisted any official sanction of dowsing techniques. The military's main objections are that the technique is not a "measurable science" or "100 percent reliable." Dowsers respond by pointing out that no military device is 100 percent reliable.

SECRET LOCATION

During the Second World War, an architect named Ludwig Straniak told German naval officers that he could pinpoint ship locations at sea simply by holding a pendulum over an admiralty chart. As a result of Straniak's claims, Adolf Hitler became intrigued by the concept of map dowsing. He was especially impressed when Straniak correctly located the battleship *Prinz Eugen* while it was on a secret voyage.

The launching of the* Prinz Eugen, *August 22, 1938

The water diviner has been an important figure among the Germanic, Anglo Saxon, and Celtic peoples for many centuries. Local "cunning men," who could both dowse and heal livestock, were part of British rural life until well into the 1800's.

Cornish roots

Dowsers took both the term and their abilities with them when they traveled to the eastern coast of America in the 16th and 17th centuries. The origin of the word *dowsing* is shrouded in mystery, but it seems to be rooted in Cornwall, England, where tin and lead miners dowsed for hidden mineral seams from pre-Christian times.

The word *dowsing* may come from the old Cornish *dewsys* meaning "goddess." The addition of *rhodi* meaning "tree branch," or "twig," results in the term *dowsing rod.* Another possible origin of the word *dowsing* is the German verb *deuten*, which can be translated variously as "to show," "to indicate," "to point out," or "to predict."

In the 16th century, miners in the Harz mountains of Germany dowsed for tin, copper, and lead using a forked

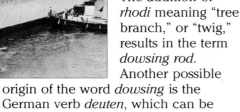

Misleading vapors
This late 17th-century French engraving shows a dowser reacting to "exhalations" rising from the ground. Dowsers and diviners, it is theorized, may respond to some unknown, and invisible, element when using their powers.

German prospectors
A 16th-century woodcut from the book De Re Metallica *shows a divining rod being used to find minerals. By the 17th and 18th centuries, the dowsing rod was considered an essential scientific instrument.*

hazel twig. The evidence for use of dowsing in Germany comes from a massive tome entitled *De Re Metallica (On Metals)* written in 1556 by an early physicist and metallurgist, Georg Bauer. In the book he described contemporary dowsing methods: "All alike grasp the forks of the twig with their hands, clenching their fists, it being necessary that the clenched fingers should be held towards the sky in order that the twig should be raised at that end where the two branches meet. Then they wander at random through mountainous regions. It is said that the moment they place their feet on a vein the twig immediately turns and twists, and so by its action discloses the vein; when they move their feet again and go away from that spot the twig once more becomes immobile."

Growing respectability

The church had often damned dowsing and divining as the work of the devil, but an exception was made for Bauer's publication. Priests read the book aloud to illiterate miners on Sundays. By the 18th century, German mineral dowsers and diviners were considered socially equal to surveyors. In the early 1900's a young American mining engineer named Herbert Clark Hoover and his wife, Lou Henry, became intrigued by *De Re Metallica* and laboriously translated the book into English. In 1912 *Mining Magazine* published the text in London. Hoover's work attracted great interest in Anglo-American mining circles. However, the mining experts were not convinced by the sections on dowsing and divining.

Both German and Cornish immigrant miners with dowsing skills had been successful in locating silver in Nevada fields, but professional geologists and mineralogists viewed the diviners with a mixture of curiosity and hostility. The translation of *De Re Metallica* made little difference to this thinking, even after Herbert Hoover became the 31st President of the United States.

When the young Hoover was publishing his translation, a new breed of prospector was searching for the dominant raw material of the 20th century — oil. Dowsers were welcomed into the oil fields, and they were given a new title, "doodlebuggers."

Modern breed

Peter Harmon explains that doodlebuggers are a breed slightly different from water diviners. "They learn to focus on oil, as we focus on water. Generally speaking, doodlebuggers use a map of the area being surveyed and the swing of a pendulum to narrow down the field. Then they may go out there in person and walk the ground with a forked stick or a pair of divining rods. Your modern doodlebugger is no witch doctor. Most of them have degrees in metallurgy or mining. Just about every major American oil company uses doodlebuggers nowadays, whether they will admit to it or not."

Although Harmon has dowsed successfully for oil and precious minerals, his full-time profession is water divining. There was no tradition of dowsing in his English/Scandinavian

Oil platform, Louisiana
Dowsing techniques are used by many oil companies.

Map dowsing
Dowsers swing a pendulum over a map to find the position of missing items.

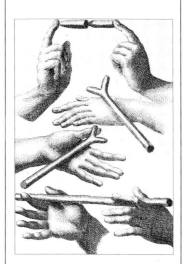

Simple apparatus
Dowsing equipment is displayed in this 18th-century French engraving.

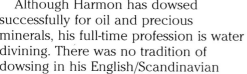

Herbert Hoover
As a mining engineer, he was intrigued by divining.

family. However, when Peter was seven, he and his friends were playing in their beechnut tree house. The tree was a long distance from home and water, and this meant that someone had to take a gallon jug and go for water twice a day. On this particular afternoon it was Peter's turn. Having returned home and filled his gallon jug with water, Peter felt a deep need to take his father's shovel and an empty barrel back to the tree house. Harmon takes up the story: "Back at the tree house I chose a site using sense and smell. When we dug a hole at that spot we found a clear spring of water. We put the wooden barrel in that spring and it filled up with water that was nice and cold and sweet. I traveled over that way recently. Although the copse is gone now, there was the old barrel with the water still bubbling up clear and cold and a frog living in it."

By the start of the 1990's, Harmon was in his late forties and was one of several hundred professional dowsers in America. For a fee he would travel anywhere in the U.S. He has also worked in Central America and Canada. "I do a

Athanasius Kircher

MYSTERIOUS TALENT

Athanasius Kircher was a Jesuit priest in the mid-17th century. He was one of the first people to theorize that a divining rod moved because of unconscious muscular movements of the diviner. It was generally believed at the time that dowsers played a passive role in their work and that external forces were responsible for movement of the divining rod.

Radiation theory

In the early 1920's, Abbé Alexis Mermet, a dowser from Savoy, France, suggested that when an object such as a dowsing rod is held over the earth, an invisible force similar to radiation shows itself through the movements of the rod. Mermet also devised an innovative map-dowsing pendulum. An item relevant to the target object or location is put in a sling at the bottom of the pendulum, which is then swung over a map of the area to be searched.

Abbé Alexis Mermet

lot of work along the Mexican border and elsewhere in the Southwest," Harmon says. "I did a job in New Mexico recently where I had to travel the last 100 miles on horseback. Then I found I couldn't get any kind of result at all, until I had rested completely. If I'm exhausted, the power or whatever it is just doesn't seem to work."

Harmon thinks the strange ability of "second-sight," as shown in the episode with the Coke bottle by the doghouse, comes to most dowsers as they develop. "The straight dowsing is there all the time. It is reliable, almost mechanical, like switching on a machine. The other 'insight' stuff comes in flashes."

In the 1980's a small business just outside of Portland, Maine, had been

Drought relief
A ground well in Niger. Dowsing has always been used as an inexpensive way of finding water sources in dry areas of poorer countries.

drilling the same well for 20 years, and its owners were desperate to find a new source of water. Fifteen dowsers joined in the search, including Harmon. He tells the story: "I was called in by the then president of the American Society of Dowsers, Norman E. Leighton. When I arrived at the site I found the driller 604 feet into the ground, but the other dowsers had given up on that hole. I had a cup of tea, and a think, and suddenly one of my 'insight' flashes sparked. I felt strongly that the hole was usable, and asked the drill operator to drill just another 43 inches through the rock. Sure enough, exactly 43 inches down, he hit clean water. I collected

my fee, and the well is still producing about 600 gallons a minute."

Peter Harmon thinks of himself as a technician. He is, in fact, skilled in the purely mechanical side of well drilling. He says: "Dowsing uses some sort of emanation or force which comes up through the earth and affects the diviner physically, causing his forked stick or rod to twitch. The instrument doesn't seem to be important, as long as there's tension there."

Sixth sense

Harmon is philosophical about his ability: "My favorite tool nowadays is a plastic-covered rod. But as you develop the skill, you develop a kind of sixth sense. If there's water around, I can

> "Dowsing uses some sort of emanation or force which comes up through the earth and affects the diviner physically, causing his forked stick or rod to twitch."

sense it, kind of 'smell' it in my mind. I think because I started dowsing pure water, I'm best at that. Others feel the same way about salt water. My ability is not in any way spooky. It's just a kinda thin tremor, and it makes me feel good. I'm not a religious man, but you could say it's a gift from God."

ASD logo
The American Society of Dowsers is an educational and scientific society with 64 local chapters.

DIVINING DEVICES

Dowsing requires only very simple equipment that you can make yourself. Many people are surprised at how successful their attempts at dowsing can be.

Traditional dowsing rod

OWSERS MAINTAIN THAT although the equipment used for dowsing plays a vital part in the experience, it is the dowser's mental attitude that is most important. The equipment, they say, merely magnifies the response that is coming from within the person who is dowsing. Scientists have found that dowsers work in a relaxed state, during which the right half of the brain seems to be dominant. This is the side of the brain that governs intuitive responses.

Making angle rods

You can make dowsing tools called angle rods from a simple pair of wire coat hangers. When dowsing, the short ends of the rods are held lightly in closed fists with the longer end uppermost, allowing the wires to rotate as freely as possible.

The rods are in a neutral position when they point straight ahead. Ideally, the dowser's fists should be tilted slightly forward, so that the rods fall naturally into the neutral position. When the rods swing across each other, this indicates that

bend outward

cut

cut

Cut and bend coat hangers to make angle rods

Angle rods

water is probably present below ground at that point.

Dowsers say that rods can locate not only water and minerals, but also buried objects and places of psychic importance, and that you must concentrate completely on visualizing whatever it is you are looking for.

The "Bishop's Rule" is used to help determine the depth at which something is buried. The rule states that the distance out from the place where you started dowsing is the depth at which whatever it is you are looking for will be found. So "distance out equals distance down" is the rough guide.

Hazel divining rod

A traditional dowsing rod can be made by cutting a forked branch about 18 to 20 inches long, $^1/_8$ to $^1/_4$ inch in diameter, from a bush or tree. Dowsers consider hazel wood to be ideal, and ash is also favored, although any wood can be used. This type of divining rod is used by holding the two top parts of the Y, with the single stem pointed away from you. Hold the two parts stretched a little apart. This makes the rod quiver slightly in your hands. The single end is then responsive to changes in pressure and movement in your body. Using the Y rod requires experience and is not as easy for a beginner to use as angle rods or a pendulum.

Wand or bobber

Another device used for dowsing is a wand, or bobber. This is made from a four-foot-long branch, about $^1/_4$ to $^1/_2$ inch in diameter. Move the wand up and down or from side to side, and walk slowly over the target area. When the wand moves in the opposite direction or in a circular motion, you have located your target.

Swinging pendulum

A small object weighing about half an ounce can be tied to the end of a piece of string 4 to 10 inches long to make a dowsing pendulum. Ideally the object should taper to a point, and the string should be made of cotton.

Practice using the pendulum by holding the string between your thumb and forefinger, about four inches above the weight. Hold your forearm parallel to the ground and relax.

Try swinging the weight so that it moves backward and forward in circles. You will soon learn the length of string that suits you best. The pendulum should feel as if it is swinging without your conscious control. Ask the pendulum questions, with clockwise or counter-clockwise movement representing certain specific answers, such as yes and no or left and right, until it responds by rotating in a definite direction.

Dowsing pendulum

How Does Dowsing Work?

Dowsers themselves often have difficulty describing how they perform their art. It is hard to establish what the source of their power might be, and there are several schools of thought on the subject.

ONE THEORY REGARDING dowsing maintains that water, and indeed all matter, emits a kind of radiation. French dowser Abbé Alexis Mermet put forward this idea in the 1920's and suggested that a dowser detects this radiation as he or she would smell a piece of ripe cheese, using some kind of obscure but natural ability. Adherents of this idea argue that man's primitive ancestors needed such a faculty to survive during periods of great drought. Various parts of the body have been mentioned as the source for this power, including the pituitary gland, the adrenal gland, and the bladder. Hence the well-known old saying "to feel something in one's water."

Another theory, supported by British writer Tom Lethbridge, held that the dowser emits radiation in the same way that bats emit high-pitched squeaks in order to navigate. The radiation bounces back from target objects in the same way that radar waves do. Lethbridge believed that this was how the sixth sense of animals operated. Observing his wife's cat, Lethbridge noted that the animal adopted an alert position before dashing outside and bringing back a mouse or vole. Experiments show that even the keen hearing of the cat could not pick up small sounds through the thick stone walls of Lethbridge's old manor house. He believed that the cat used its whiskers as tiny divining rods.

Superconsciousness

Yet another school of thought, attracting an increasing number of both dowsers and parapsychologists, is that divining depends on a "superconsciousness." The supporters of this theory believe that the ability surfaces in all of us from time to time. For example, when a

On target
Tom Lethbridge thought dowsers emit radiation that bounces off objects in much the same way as radar.

Lethbridge believed that the cat used its whiskers as tiny divining rods.

Sixth sense
According to Tom Lethbridge, a cat suddenly springing to catch a mouse may be using an innate dowsing ability.

Spring siting
Megaliths are often built on the site of blind, underground, springs.

POWER POINTS

Englishman Guy Underwood was a dowser for over 20 years before his death in 1964. He believed that there are paths of power over the earth called geodetic lines. He mapped these into patterns and called them the earth force.

Underwood thought that these lines were recognized by our ancestors and are felt by plants and animals as well. He found that blind springs were located at points where the primary lines of his system converge. Many megalithic monuments are found over blind springs. Underwood pointed out that badgers also make their burrows over these springs, and yews grow best above them.

Animal cunning
Badgers seem to sense the location of underground springs and build burrows over them.

Tree sensitivity
Something within a yew tree may be linked to forces beneath the earth.

telephone rings and we just "sense" who is calling before we answer. People in dangerous professions — miners, deep-sea divers, firefighters — often develop an inexplicable "sixth sense" that warns them of impending peril. It may be that some similar "superconscious" talent accounts for the ability of dowsers.

Many dowsers believe that their abilities could be explained by a combination of theories, and that when some form of radiations below ground are sensed by a dowser, they cause a tiny tic in certain muscles of the dowser's body. Dr. Jan Merta de Velehrad, a Czech-born physiologist and psychologist, was based at McGill University in Montreal during the 1970's. Dr. Merta de Velehrad thought that the movement of the dowsing rod or wand was directly connected to minute muscular contractions, found principally in the wrist area. These movements become more noticeable when they were transferred to the dowsing rod or wand. Dr. Merta de Velehrad constructed a measuring instrument, called an accelerometer, which recorded a subject dowser's muscular contractions in relation to the motions of his or her dowsing rod. Dr. Merta de Velehrad found that the interval between the muscle contraction

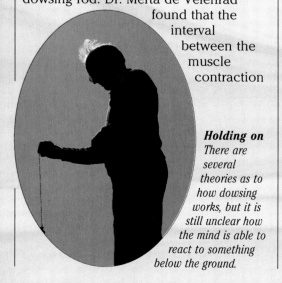

Hand dowsing
Colin Bloy relies solely on muscular responses while dowsing at the Merry Maidens stone circle, Land's End, Cornwall.

Holding on
There are several theories as to how dowsing works, but it is still unclear how the mind is able to react to something below the ground.

and the rod's movement was about half a second. He concluded that a dowser's muscular contractions were a physical manifestation of his or her reaction to hidden elements. After many experiments, Dr. Merta de Velehrad decided that dowsers who can pick up impulses without using dowsing devices are simply paying close attention to movements that usually pass unnoticed.

Maine dowser Peter Harmon has developed some innovative new dowsing techniques but remains unsure of how they really work. He has constructed a 12-foot metal tube, with a hole like the mouthpiece of a giant whistle, which he uses as a depth sounder when seeking water. "I stick it into the ground at my selected spot, and concentrate," he says. "The tube seems to act as a subsonic organ pipe, giving off vibrations which I feel rather than hear. I've learned to 'read' the vibrations in terms of depth. It's amazingly accurate, but quite frankly, it frightens me in a strange way. It's so unlike any of my other 'dowsing' reactions. I have no idea how it works."

Orthodox scientists are skeptical of the whole dowsing phenomenon. Like other aspects of the paranormal, divining does not show up well under laboratory conditions. Magician James Randi has offered a $10,000 reward to any dowser who can produce results under test conditions. By the early 1990's no diviner had satisfied Randi's stringent criteria.

The British Ministry of Defence has also dismissed dowsing techniques. In 1971 the ministry's scientists observed a team of 22 dowsers as they attempted to locate metal, plastic, concrete, wood, and water in an exhaustive series of experiments. The ministry report concluded: "That there is no real evidence of any dowsing ability which could produce results better than chance or guessing."

Dr. Jan Merta de Velehrad
Dr. Merta de Velehrad has shown a link between muscle contractions and the movements of dowsing rods.

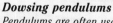

Dowsing pendulums
Pendulums are often used by dowsers to pinpoint locations on maps before they actually travel to the area to investigate further.

A criminal
always leaves
something at the
scene of a crime
and, conversely,
takes something
away.

THE PSYCHIC DETECTIVES

Criminals take every precaution to avoid leaving clues at the scene of a crime. But they may unwittingly leave an invisible trail that can be uncovered by investigators with an unexpected talent.

*L*ATE IN OCTOBER 1978, seven-year-old Carl Carter was missing from his Los Angeles home. There were no clues, and the police were unsure as to whether the boy had simply wandered off or had been abducted. After some days, the boy still had not been found. A retired police officer friend of the Carter family suggested consulting a psychometrist. A psychometrist is a diviner who reads impressions from objects associated with absent people or things. A psychic, known simply as Joan, was consulted because she had had previous minor successes with police work.

Psychic Joan

After handling clothing belonging to the missing boy, Joan told police that he was dead and described his murderer. A police artist sketched the killer based on Joan's description. On seeing the picture, Carl's father said, "That looks like Butch."

"Butch" Memro

He was referring to Harold Ray "Butch" Memro, a friend of the Carter family. Memro was arrested and confessed not only to strangling Carl, but also to killing two other boys during the past two years. At Memro's trial, his lawyer moved that the case be dismissed on the grounds that the prosecution's case was based solely on psychic evidence. The judge overruled him, thereby setting a legal precedent.

Trace remains

At the beginning of the 20th century, the Belgian criminologist Prof. Edmund Locard put forward the basis of forensic science: "Every contact leaves a trace." This implies that a criminal always leaves something at the scene of a crime and, conversely, takes something away.

Artist's sketch of the murderer

Ginette Matacia

PRIVATE INVESTIGATOR

Ginette Matacia is a Virginia psychic. She began dowsing as a young child with her father, Louis, who is a professional dowser. Ginette is the only known psychic detective in the U.S. with a private investigator's registration. As well as helping the public on private matters, she has also been consulted by the police. Ginette has used her psychic talents to help distraught parents find missing children.

MURDEROUS IMPRESSIONS

In 1958, when he was 49, Gerard Croiset was a subject at the Parapsychology Institute of the University of Utrecht. He was given a pair of red slippers and asked to say what impressions he received from them. Croiset said that the slippers belonged to a pretty, young woman who had been murdered in her American home by a bushy-haired man. Croiset drew accurate sketches of the woman and her home.

Strong convictions

The slippers studied by Croiset belonged to Marilyn Sheppard, who was murdered in her home outside Cleveland in July 1954. Her husband, Dr. Sam Sheppard, was convicted of the crime.

Dr. Sam Sheppard (right), with his attorney

Dr. Sheppard maintained that an unknown bushy-haired man had knocked him unconscious and killed his wife. Croiset supported Dr. Sheppard's claim. In the early 1960's Croiset still insisted: "The bushy-haired man did it — not her husband! I am absolutely sure."

A murderer may leave a bullet in his victim's body and take away a splash of blood. Police rely on material left at the scene of a crime to give them clues about possible suspects. Psychometrists claim that the same principle applies to "psychic" detection.

Psychometrists believe that every piece of clothing belonging to a murder victim carries extrasensory "impressions" beyond those belonging to victim and killer. Such items may also hold confusing impressions of whoever made the clothing or the employee who sold it.

Yorkshire Ripper

Although most sensational murders attract a variety of hints from psychics, the suggestions are rarely useful. The Yorkshire Ripper was a killer who attacked women in the north of England during the late 1970's. The case attracted dozens of would-be psychic detectives, few of whom were anywhere near the target. One exception was the London-based psychometrist Robert Cracknell.

In early November 1980 Cracknell gave the police a detailed description of a house in Bradford, West Yorkshire, which he said was the home of the Ripper. Cracknell predicted that the killer would strike only once more, in about a fortnight, and would be caught "fairly soon" after that crime.

The Ripper's last victim was Jacqueline Hill, who was murdered on November 17, 1980. On January 4, 1981, police arrested Peter Sutcliffe. He was subsequently convicted of the Ripper killings and sentenced to life imprisonment. Pictures of Sutcliffe's Bradford house reportedly tallied closely with the description Cracknell had given some time earlier.

Perhaps the most famous "psychic detectives" of the 20th century have been Dutchmen Gerard Croiset and Peter Hurkos. During their lives, the two men were praised by the American and European press as near miracle workers. Gerard Croiset was born in 1909 and had a difficult childhood. Abandoned by his

Robert Cracknell

parents, he was brought up in a series of foster homes before setting out to make his living in menial jobs. By the 1930's Croiset had developed abilities as a psychic healer and had experienced some success at finding missing people. The Dutch police occasionally sought his guidance, and as a result Croiset's reputation spread to the United States.

However, he preferred not to leave Holland, and his normal method of working was to ask that material relating to a victim be sent to him.

One of Croiset's successes involved a missing person case in 1961. On February 22 a four-year-old girl named Edith Kiecorius disappeared from her home in Brooklyn. When she had not been found three days later, an official of the Dutch airline KLM offered to fly Croiset to New York to join the search. Instead, Croiset asked the police to send him a photo of Edith, a map of the city, and an item of her clothing.

Remote sensing

When he had studied the various items sent by the police, Croiset felt sure that the girl had been murdered. He described a gray building that he thought had five stories, the second of which gave him "strong emotion." He said the building was near a river and an elevated railway, and had a billboard on top. Croiset thought the murderer was wearing gray, came from southern Europe, and was in his mid-fifties. Soon after Croiset telephoned his descriptions to New York, the police were involved in a routine search of an area on the banks of the Hudson River. An elevated railway ran nearby. Although the search was not connected with Edith's disappearance, the police found her body in a room on the second floor of a gray building. The landlord described the occupant as a middle-aged European. The police made a swift arrest.

In the case of Edith's murder, Croiset was undoubtedly accurate in some crucial respects, but there were also a

Helping the police
Gerard Croiset (left), studies details of a crime and offers his psychic impressions.

number of inaccuracies. The building in which the body was discovered was four, not five, stories high, and there was no billboard on top. The killer was from England, not southern Europe.

Peter Hurkos, who was two years younger than Croiset, had an uneventful childhood and showed no interest in or aptitude for psychic matters until he was 30. Then, on July 10, 1941, Hurkos apparently experienced a remarkable case of premonition after he fell four stories while working as a house painter in The Hague. He was unconscious for four days. When he woke, his first words were to his wife: "Bea, what are you doing here? Where's Benny? The room is burning." Five days later, the couple's son Benny was trapped in a burning building and was rescued just in time.

According to Hurkos, his psychic powers developed rapidly following his accident. After the war, Hurkos used his new "mind-reading" powers to enter show business. In 1948 he moved to Hollywood and became a popular psychic to a number of stars.

In June 1957 Peter Hurkos was involved in a particularly tragic case. The 10-year-old daughter of a close friend of his named Henry Belk had vanished while playing in the woods in North Carolina. Belk asked Hurkos for assistance. Hurkos had a vision of the child lying face down in six feet of water, near a boathouse. Searchers quickly identified the boathouse, and found the girl's body. Belk's reaction was extremely bitter: "If Hurkos can see the future, why didn't he warn me?"

A year later, Hurkos had another success. In Miami he helped solve the murder of a taxi driver who had been shot. Hurkos sat in the murdered man's cab and had a vision of a tall, skinny man with a tattoo on his right arm. Hurkos said the pistol found in the cab had been used to kill another man earlier that night. With the help of information supplied by Hurkos, the police were able to charge a man called Charles Smith with both of the Miami murders.

Unfortunately, most tips Hurkos gave did not lead to arrests. In 1964 he attempted to help the authorities find the notorious Boston Strangler who had brutally murdered 13 women.

Although no one was ever convicted of the crime, police came to the conclusion that Alberto De Salvo, who was arrested for a different series of attacks, had committed the Boston murders. Hurkos disagreed — he maintained that a man who police referred to as Thomas P. O'Brien was the real Strangler. Both De Salvo and O'Brien ended up in mental hospitals, where they were immune to prosecution. The Boston Strangler case was closed without even coming to trial.

Convicted murderer Albert De Salvo (left)

CRIME OF PASSION

In 1947 Peter Hurkos claimed that he helped police in the Dutch province of Limburg to solve the mystery of a fatal shooting. The victim was a young coal miner named van Tossing. After holding the miner's coat, Hurkos told the police that the murderer was the miner's stepfather. Hurkos said the stepfather was in love with the murdered man's wife and that the murder weapon could be found on the roof of the dead man's house. The gun *was* found in the gutter of the roof, and fingerprints led to the conviction of the miner's stepfather, Bernard van Tossing.

Actor Albert Salmi and Peter Hurkos (right)

PSYCHIC ARCHEOLOGY

Many archeologists have approached dowsing with an open mind. As a result, dowsers and diviners are using their psychic skills to help in the search for the hidden past of humankind.

IN THE EARLY 1970's Dr. J. Norman Emerson was one of Canada's most eminent archeologists and president of the Canadian Archaeological Association. He became impressed by the talents of dowser George McMullen and decided to test his unusual abilities. McMullen practiced a specialized form of dowsing and divining known as psychometry. By using his psychometric talents, McMullen said that he was able to sense historical impressions from ancient objects.

At a meeting of the Canadian Archaeological Association in 1973, McMullen was handed a crudely

Dr. J. Norman Emerson

carved piece of black stone. The stone had been found on an ancient Indian site in the Queen Charlotte Islands, off the coast of British Columbia. McMullen felt that the stone had been carved by a native of West Africa. McMullen said the carver was a slave who had been transported to the Caribbean, where he worked for a time. The slave was then sold to an Englishman and taken on a ship to the west coast of North America, where he managed to escape from his captors and join a group of Indians.

By coincidence, when the archeological society's meeting was taking place, one of Dr. Emerson's graduate students was working at the Royal Ontario Museum cataloging artifacts from West Africa. Emerson asked the student to examine the carved stone. The student recognized it to be of the same origin as a number of masks from Sierra Leone, which he had seen at the museum. These observations lent some support to McMullen's claim that the stone from the Indian site had been carved by a native of West Africa.

Archeologists have cooperated with dowsers on a variety of

Glastonbury Abbey

One of the earliest examples of psychic archeology concerns Glastonbury Abbey in England. In 1907, the abbey ruins were bought by the nation and architect Frederick Bligh Bond was appointed to direct excavations. Bond asked a psychic, John Bartlett, to help in the search for two old chapels.

Bartlett produced a plan of the abbey, based on communications he had received from spirits. When workmen dug where Bartlett indicated, the chapels and a skeleton and a skull were unearthed. Bartlett said that the skeleton was Ralph the Chancellor and the skull belonged to Eawulf the Saxon, whom Ralph had slain in a fight.

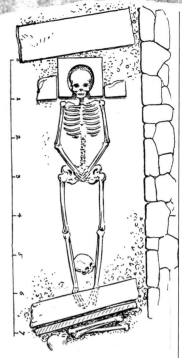

Grave matter
Psychic archeologist Umberto di Grazia claimed to have used his powers to discover this Etruscan grave in Italy.

Champlain and his Iroquois allies confront the enemy
In 1974 Dr. J. Norman Emerson gave psychic Fran Farley a piece of metal to study. Farley said she could see white men and Indians. Dr. Emerson then reportedly revealed that the metal was from a kettle which Samuel de Champlain, the founder of Quebec, gave to Iroquois Indians in return for help.

projects. David E. Jones, an American university teacher of anthropology, became intrigued by psychic archeology in the late 1960's. As an experiment, Jones gave stones to three psychics and asked them to describe their origins. Although the Mayan origins of the stones were known, Jones himself was not aware of them; so there was no way he could have transferred information to the psychics. The three psychics reportedly described the stones as originating from Mayan sites. Jones was amazed: "Those nondescript stones could just as easily have come from an Eskimo site in Greenland, a Bedouin site in Yemen, or a Papuan site in highland New Guinea."

Early foundations

The most convincing evidence for psychic archeology may be found in *Dowsing and Church Archaeology* published in 1987. The authors include English academics Richard Bailey, professor of Anglo-Saxon civilization at the University of Newcastle, and Eric Cambridge, research assistant working in the Department of Archeology, at the University of Durham. The third author, dowser and diviner Denis Briggs, is a retired engineer.

Revealing objects
Just by grasping an object such as this Cro-Magnon sculpture of a woman, psychometrists claim to be able to describe its origins.

Briggs knew that many of the Saxon and early medieval churches in the northeastern section of England are actually set on foundations that are much older. Primitive chapels of wood and plaster had been built on these sites by early Christians. In 1981 Briggs dowsed a sample of 44 churches, from tiny chapels to cathedrals, and drew up plans of the earlier foundations that had been revealed by his divining.

"I used rods made from coat hangers, and thought of architectural plans in my mind," said Briggs.

Prof. Bailey and Dr. Cambridge were impressed by the information supplied by Briggs, but skeptical of his methods. So they sought permission from individual church authorities to excavate in order to check out unusual features in Briggs's descriptions. They checked only details that bore no relation to any visible structural features or that had not appeared on any plans, no matter how remote or inaccessible.

Prof. Bailey and Dr. Cambridge were impressed by the results. Time and time again they found that Briggs's predictions of what they would find were accurate to the inch. But what astounded them most was his ability to trace things that were no longer there — a process known as "remanence" or psychic imprinting.

For example, at St. Mary's Church in Ponteland, Briggs insisted on tracing a rectangular feature in the altar area. Excavation showed nothing to back up this claim. But then obscure plans were found that revealed that a wooden altar platform with steps had been put down on the space in Victorian times. This altar had been taken up in the early 1970's.

Prof. Bailey, who prefers to think that dowsers pick up on some kind of disturbance in the soil, did not like this idea of psychic imprinting. "I find the most difficulty in swallowing that side of it," he says. "What I want to believe is that you are getting a physical response to a physical problem. But imprinting seems to be linked to something else. It seems much closer to what sounds like a kind of psychical phenomenon."

Grains of truth
"Sand-reading" is a method used by psychometrists to discover a person's past or future. They read the impression made in the sand by a client's hand.

PSYCHOMETRY

Psychometry is thought to be a form of ESP by which dowsers receive impressions about people, events, and places by studying related objects.

In 1902, American author and lecturer Thomas Jay Hudson defined psychometry as "the supposed power of the human mind to discern the history of inanimate objects by clairvoyance."

One of the first observers of psychometry was the French psychical researcher Eugene Osty. He published his findings in 1923 in a book called *Supernormal Faculties in Man*. Osty noted that some of the best psychometrists needed only the slightest contact with their target object. They claim that handling a book flipped through by an absent person, or sitting in a chair once occupied by him or her, would be sufficient to produce related information.

CHAPTER FIVE

MIND OVER MATTER

Can the mind influence matter from a distance? The idea sounds impossible, but strange happenings, from bent spoons and floating furniture to stopped clocks and psychic photographs, leave many people convinced that the phenomenon known as psychokinesis is real.

We all try to influence matter in our everyday lives, probably without even realizing that this is what we are doing. Golfers contort themselves while urging a ball to change direction if they have hit it off course. Gamblers try to persuade dice to land a certain way. Someone hoping for a phone call tries to will the phone to ring. If actions of this kind are successful the implication is that we are influencing matter with our minds — a phenomenon

A MATTER OF TIME

Clocks and watches stopping at the moment of death are a fairly common phenomenon, one that remains unexplained. Some stories tell of timepieces actually starting at a time of crisis rather than coming to a halt. The following example was reported by Louisa Rhine in her book *ESP in Life and Lab* (1967):

"My father had a younger brother, Ben, who fought in the Second World War. On their farm in Missouri they had an old grandfather's clock that had not run for many years. One day the old clock began to run as though nothing had ever been wrong with it. At the same time Ben's devoted shepherd dog began to howl. This howling continued all day.

"A few days later the family received a telegram from the War Department. Ben had been killed in action at Aachen, Germany, on November 29, 1944. This was the day the clock started and Ben's dog howled."

known as psychokinesis (PK). One possible example of mind over matter that has been reported consistently over the years is the unexpected and mysterious stopping of a clock at the time of a person's death. Of course it is possible that such events happen simply by chance. But many people who have witnessed these timely breakdowns believe that the dead are responsible for them, and are trying to draw attention to their passing or attempting to prove that some force continues beyond the grave.

Alternatively, the phenomenon might be explained by a combination of telepathy and PK. At the moment of death, a friend or relative of the

The clock stopped at the exact time the woman's mother died.

deceased may "receive" the terrible news subconsciously, and the psychic trauma that results might have sufficient power to stop the hands of a clock.

The following incident was reported by a woman from Illinois to parapsychologist Louisa Rhine, who recorded it along with many similar stories in her book *ESP in Life and Lab* (1967). In 1952 a 100-year-old clock stopped at the exact time the woman's mother died. Although the timepiece was rewound, it stopped the next day at precisely the same time.

The clock continued to work without problems until three years later, when it stopped at the very moment that the woman's eldest daughter gave birth to her first child. The next day it stopped at that same time again. Was it coincidence or PK — or something else — that stopped a clock that had been in a family for generations?

Nina Kulagina

There are people who claim to demonstrate a deliberate power of mind over matter, and considerable research into such claims has been carried out worldwide. Nina Kulagina was a Russian housewife who was tested in the 1960's by parapsychologist L. L. Vasiliev at the Institute of Brain Research in Leningrad. Kulagina convinced Vasiliev that she could move objects, including the hands of clocks, without even touching them.

In the early 1980's Chinese scientist Zhou Peiyuan, formerly Peking University president and more recently chairman of the Chinese Science and Technology Association, was among several scientists who witnessed a PK demonstration in Peking by four young students from the Kunming Yunnan Province. The students could apparently make objects move simply by focusing their thoughts on them.

In 1984 a Japanese TV crew devoted a week to filming Polish

Trying conditions
In 1989 researchers noted that Monica Nieto Tegada, a 15-year-old Spanish girl, seemed to bend a metal strip inside a sealed glass container, simply by concentrating on it.

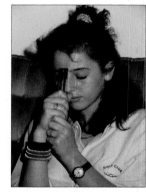

Source of power
Mind power may be able to twist and curl metal with incredible force.

teenager Joasia Gajewski in an attempt to record her alleged powers of PK. Gajewski's strange ability to influence inanimate objects was first noticed when light bulbs started to explode whenever she entered a room. The film crew's patience was rewarded when they captured the flight of a fork across a room — and were unable to find an obvious natural explanation for the sudden movement.

Bottled PK
In 1978 researchers at the Society for Research on Rapport and Telekinesis (SORRAT) in Columbia, Missouri, reported that subject Joe Mangini used PK to bend a spoon while it was sealed inside a bottle.

In another case, a Brazilian woman, Aglae Moreira da Silva, is said by physics professor Carlos Antonio Porta to be able to use her PK powers not to shatter bulbs, but to make them light. The professor conducted a series of tests with Silva in the 1980's. "I designed an apparatus with a 1.5 volt bulb connected to wires," Porta reported, "I placed it on her hand....the light flickered and then stayed lit."

These stories of psychic wonders are not a modern phenomenon. More than a century ago scientists were already investigating the extraordinary PK powers of physical mediums such as Daniel Dunglas Home (a Scottish-American), Eusapia Palladino (an Italian), and Stanislawa Tomczyk (a Pole).

In Home's presence, according to many accounts, events took place for which there seemed to be no natural cause. Musical instruments would play, tables rose into the air, and Home himself was

Flexible talent
A fork distorted during a metal-bending experiment may be showing the potential of mind over matter.

said to levitate. He was investigated in the 1870's by Sir William Crookes, an eminent British scientist, and Crookes became convinced that Home's PK ability was authentic.

Palladino was studied extensively in the late 1800's by a commission set up in Milan. In 1892 the commission declared that she was genuine: "It is impossible to count the number of times that a hand appeared and was touched by one of us. Suffice it to say that doubt was no longer possible. It was indeed a

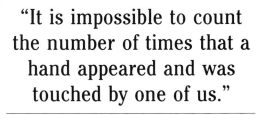

> ## "It is impossible to count the number of times that a hand appeared and was touched by one of us."

living, human hand which we saw and touched, while at the same time the bust and arms of the medium were visible and her hands were held and controlled on either side."

In the early 1900's, Tomczyk demonstrated her apparent talent to levitate and move small objects by holding her hands around them. She was studied by eminent psychologist Dr. Julien Ochorowicz, who believed that she was not a fraud.

Dr. Ochorowicz felt that Tomczyk's ability to move objects was caused by tiny, spiderweb-like threads that emanated naturally from her hands and connected to the objects which she appeared to levitate. "When the medium separates her hands," Ochorowicz stated in one of several reports he wrote concerning Tomczyk, "the thread gets thinner and disappears....It can be photographed and is then seen to be much thinner than an ordinary thread. Needless to remark that the hands of the medium were examined carefully before every experiment."

What can be the explanation for these effects? Fraud certainly does take place — but as we learn more about the nature of the universe and the power of the mind, PK remains a possibility.

Suspended blades
Stanislawa Tomczyk appears to levitate a pair of scissors.

GREAT MEDIUMS

Stanislawa Tomczyk was a Polish psychic whose "powers" were discovered in 1909. She reportedly placed her hands around objects which then rose as she raised her hands.

Twenty years before Tomczyk came to prominence, one of the

Eusapia Palladino

greatest mediums was a small Italian woman called Eusapia Palladino. She was born in 1854 and seemed capable of stimulating psychic phenomena even as a child. Cesare Lombroso, a famous Italian psychiatrist, tested Palladino in 1888 and subsequently devoted much of his life to psychic research.

Impressive test

Palladino's most intriguing feat was her reported ability to impress finger marks in a dish of putty. According to Lombroso she did this from a distance while her hands and feet were under constant observation.

AMAZING SCIENCE

> "Most physicists find it impossible to discuss subatomic processes without using adjectives like bizarre. Little wonder that parapsychologists feel a natural affinity with this branch of science."
> Scientist Danah Zohar, *Through the Time Barrier*

> "The microphysical world of the atom exhibits certain features whose affinities with the psychic have impressed themselves even on the physicists."
> Swiss psychologist Carl Gustav Jung

MANY PEOPLE DISCOUNT PSYCHOKINESIS (PK) and other paranormal phenomena on the grounds that their very existence is contrary not only to common sense, but also to the laws of physics. These non-believers argue that such events must be the result of misidentification, fraud, or chance, since acceptance of the idea that human minds may influence objects at a distance would require a new scientific model of our world and the universe.

Yet there are scientists who believe that many supposedly paranormal happenings can be explained within the framework of our current scientific knowledge. Furthermore, some of the realities of modern physics seem nearly as bizarre and intriguing as the most obscure of "psychic" occurrences.

Subatomic world

Drawn up by Isaac Newton (1642–1727), the principles of classical physics were based on the idea of cause and effect — if all conditions are known at any given time, the outcome of any situation can be predicted. This theory is generally sound, but only when dealing with the behavior of objects larger than the atom.

For a long time after its existence was postulated by the Greek philosopher Leucippus in the fifth century B.C., the atom was considered the smallest building block of matter; indeed, our word "atom" derives from the Greek *atomos*, meaning indivisible.

However, at the beginning of the 20th century, scientists began to discover and explore the structure and behavior of the particles that make up the atom (what is known as the subatomic world), and the emission of radiation within it. In 1900, a German physicist named Max Planck theorized that such radiation is emitted in small packets of energy called quanta, and thus the name for the study of this new realm — quantum mechanics — was born.

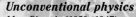

Unconventional physics
Max Planck (1858–1947) provided the basic concepts leading to quantum theory. He was awarded the Nobel Prize in physics in 1918 for his work. Quantum mechanics studies events at a subatomic level, events that are very different from both our everyday experience and conventional physics.

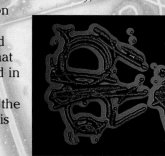

Particle collision
Photographic color enhancement of an electronic image enables us to see the debris following a collision between subatomic particles.

Building blocks
Through dedicated and ever more complex research, scientists are discovering more about the components of the universe. This artificial cube-like image shows some of the minuscule particles that form our world.

Not surprisingly, quantum mechanics revolutionized physics. For in the light of this new knowledge, several previously unshakable convictions had to be reconsidered. For example, it had been assumed that an object could only be in one place at a time, yet subatomic particles can occupy several positions simultaneously. Thus it is the essentially unpredictable nature of quantum mechanics that sets it apart from classical physics, and may link it to the paranormal.

Subatomic symmetry
Observation at a subatomic level has revealed inexplicable links between particles.

Similarly, traditionally science denied that one object could influence another from a distance without any obvious connection. Yet two photons (minute amounts of radiant energy) may go off in different directions, and when scientists measure photon X and photon Y and note their spins, they find that they are exactly opposite — no matter where the photons are. It is as if X knows what Y is doing. This might explain, paranormal enthusiasts suggest, how people suddenly "know" things about a disaster happening far away; there may be no communication in the macro (larger than atomic) world with which we are all familiar, but subtler connections at the subatomic level might be responsible.

Weird links

American physicists Evan Harris Walker and German-born Helmut Schmidt are among those who have put forward "observation theories" linking psi phenomena and quantum physics. Walker has described consciousness as the brain linking with the external world via the senses to form a kind of quantum mechanical system.

Another change in modern physics that has affected thinking about paranormal phenomena involves Albert Einstein's theories of relativity. These outline new ways of measuring and studying time and space that are based on the idea that everything is relative,

and each observer records the same event differently.

One of Einstein's theories, the General Theory of Relativity (1915), suggested the notion that space itself is curved. In 1949, mathematician Kurt Gödel produced a cosmological model showing that if space is curved, then so is time. Gödel's idea is clearly not proven, but if it were true, then the Newtonian assumption that the past and the present influence the future might not always be true — instead time might move in a circle, so that the future might also influence the past and the present. In the same way, we could not speak of "before" and "after," because these terms would have no real meaning. In addition, Gödel suggested that to travel into the future we would need to fly in the direction of the earth's rotation; to return to the past we would need to fly against it.

Spooky connections

Whatever the ultimate nature of reality, it seems at least that everything in the universe might be connected in ways that we do not yet fully comprehend. Before quantum physics and relativity theories, scientists generally regarded bizarre ideas about knowing the future (and other, related, phenomena) as totally unscientific and completely absurd. Yet modern discoveries suggest that psychic phenomena might have some scientific basis after all. For example, the French experimental physicist Alain Aspect wrote that, "the strangeness of the quantum world, including the spooky action at a distance that Einstein hated, is correct." (*New Scientist*, November 1990.)

EINSTEIN'S THEORIES
Albert Einstein (1879–1955) developed theories of relativity which opened entirely new ways of seeing time and space.

For a long time, Einstein rejected the idea of hypothetical time travel. He insisted at first that it was impossible — but he was surprisingly sympathetic when mathematician Kurt Gödel published his ideas hypothesizing that a moment "now" could be simultaneous with a time in the "future" or one in the "past." Einstein came to accept the possibility of time reversibility as a result of what quantum physics had revealed.

Psychic puzzle
This dramatic tangle of paper clips appeared to be bent by the PK powers of children in Prof. John Hasted's University of London laboratory. Such a result seems unscientific and could be some kind of fraud. Yet, aspects of modern physics we now believe to be true are just as fantastic.

Prof. John Hasted

TIRELESS INVESTIGATIONS

The work of the investigating teams based at Duke University in Durham, North Carolina, is mentioned — of necessity — whenever ESP and PK are discussed. The most renowned of these investigators, Dr. J. B. Rhine, has been called the father of modern parapsychology. He and his wife, Louisa, studied botany at the University of Chicago soon after the First World War. But it was not until 1922 that Dr. Rhine's interest in the paranormal began after he attended a lecture by Sir Arthur Conan Doyle, author of the Sherlock Holmes stories, which considered a reality beyond the material world.

By the late 1920's psychologist William McDougall moved from Harvard to Duke University where he established the nation's first

Dr. J. B. and Louisa Rhine

university parapsychology laboratory, and Dr. Rhine was appointed as its first director. The laboratory was initially part of the psychology department, but the university subsequently decided that work on ESP should be kept apart from more conventional studies, and by the early 1950's the laboratory was operating independently.

The nature of man

Dr. Rhine went on to set up an independent research facility, the Foundation for Research on the Nature of Man, and in 1965 the foundation's Institute for Parapsychology took over the work of the Duke laboratory. Dr. Rhine died in 1980, after a psychic research career that had inspired both hostility and admiration.

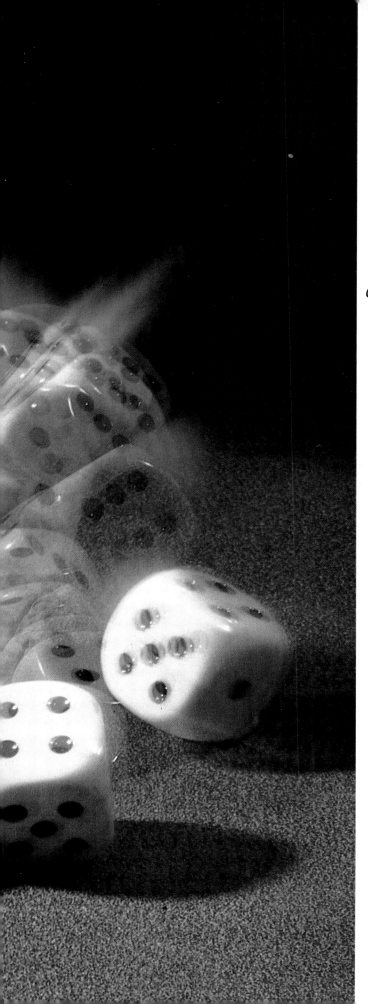

THE DICE ARE LOADED

Some gamblers believe that when they hit a lucky streak, they have an inexplicable power over the dice and just can't lose. These claims might have a real basis in the mysterious realm of psychokinesis.

"HEY, DOC, I'VE GOT SOMETHING to tell you I think you ought to know." These were the words of a professional gambler as he strolled into Dr. J. B. Rhine's parapsychology laboratory at Duke University one day in 1934. The gambler had noticed that if he was in a special state of heightened concentration while involved in a dice game, the dice would land exactly as he wanted them to fall. He was certain that he could influence his chances of winning just by using positive thoughts. Dr. Rhine was intrigued by what the gambler had to say, and within a few minutes the two men were on the floor rolling dice.

Dr. Rhine had just completed a series of experiments in extrasensory perception (ESP), and was ready for a new challenge. Eager to test the wider influence of psychic powers on our lives, Dr. Rhine began informal laboratory tests on psychokinesis (PK) with dice. Although the results with the young gambler were not recorded, the parapsychologist was sufficiently impressed by what he had seen to try experiments with other people under somewhat more rigorous conditions. So it was that laboratory research into psychokinesis began, almost by chance.

Lucky throws

Dr. Rhine and his wife, Louisa, were among the 25 participants in the first tests. They simply threw two dice against a wall, willing them to land so that together the two uppermost faces totaled seven. Twelve throws constituted what they called a "run."

The results appeared to be significant. A total of 562 runs were made, which should have produced 2,810 successes, called "hits," if only chance were operating. However, Dr. Rhine's subjects had more than 3,100 hits. The odds against this, they said, were 1 billion to 1.

Was it PK at work, or had the subjects developed a special skill in throwing dice? To overcome this doubt, Dr. Rhine devised a very simple dice-throwing machine. It consisted of a board with corrugated cardboard stuck to it. The board rested at a 45° angle on a chair. The dice were balanced on a ruler held at

CAUSE AND EFFECT

PK tests using dice show that scoring rates are not affected by how much the dice weigh or the material used to make them. This supports the view that the force responsible is not physiological.

However, while variations in the actual dice are not important, researchers believe that the randomness in how they are thrown *does* seem to affect PK. The more bounces of the dice, the more random the throw, and the greater the possible PK effect.

the top of the board and the subject then pulled the ruler away, causing the dice to roll down the board. It was impossible to influence the movement physically. In 108 runs on this device, the success rate was as far above chance as in tests using dice thrown by hand.

To rule out the possibility that the dice were biased, Dr. Rhine varied the numbers used as targets. But the results produced were still above chance. However, when the goal was a series of throws aiming at a mixture of low and

---

"The significance was so great that we were at last fully convinced that the PK effect was real."

---

high combinations, the results were merely in line with chance. Dr. Rhine felt this reflected the aversion of some of the subjects to throwing low number scores.

Special effect

Another unexpected pattern found in the test results was discovered when one of Dr. Rhine's laboratory helpers, Betty Humphrey, began analyzing some of the data in the early 1940's. It was discovered that subjects taking part in the dice-rolling experiments produced far better results in the first quarter of the tests than the last quarter. This effect, known as quarter distribution (QD), occurred throughout. The suggestion of this QD effect is that people are better able to produce PK effects early on in an experiment when they are fresh and able to concentrate most. Dr. Rhine himself had discovered a similar effect in his earlier ESP tests. In 1954, he wrote in *New World of the Mind*: "The significance of this hit distribution data, found long after the tests had been made, was so great that we were at last fully convinced that the PK effect was real."

Dr. Rhine did not publish the results of his first PK tests until nearly 10 years after he began his first experiments — the report appeared in the *Journal of*

Parapsychology in 1943. That same year, Dr. Rhine was approached by a divinity student, William Gatling, who was interested in psi research. Gatling believed that ESP, and especially PK, might have something in common with the power of prayer.

Prayer vs. PK

Dr. Rhine was intrigued by the suggestion and set up an experiment in which Gatling and three other divinity students prayed in an attempt to influence the dice. Meanwhile, another four students known for their crap-shooting success tried using PK.

The experiment was competitive, with each group trying to obtain a higher score than the other by throwing six dice and trying to influence them to land with a specific face uppermost. Both groups managed similar results, scoring well above chance after 1,242 runs. The gamblers recorded an average score of 4.52, and the divinity students achieved 4.51 against a chance expectation of 4. Their combined result produced impressive odds, Dr. Rhine reported, of billions to one.

Manual test
The first Duke trials involved throwing dice by hand.

Other researchers soon set about trying to replicate the results and introduced their own refinements. Laura Dale, a research assistant at the American Society for Psychical Research in New York, used 54 college students as her dice-throwing subjects. An elevated ledge, dice, and a plank with corrugated baffles were used for her experiments to ensure that the subjects could not physically throw the dice in a way that would influence their fall. Each subject was asked to launch the dice 96 times and to try to produce a target number.

The subjects then threw the dice 96 more times, trying to make them land with a different face as the target. The task was repeated

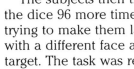

until all six faces of the dice had been selected. All six faces were used as targets to rule out the concern that the

Shaking cubes
Some early PK trials at Duke University used mechanical shakers. One particular test involved two subjects having a "tug of wills," during which each person tried to make a different side of the dice appear uppermost.

dice were loaded or "biased" in any possible way. In this way the experiment covered 31,104 readings. Dale's subjects achieved 171 more direct hits than predicted by chance, and they also scored equally well on any of the six faces. Interestingly, those who believed in PK were found to achieve better results than skeptics. The group also scored more hits at the beginning of each run, confirming the QD effect discovered at Duke University.

Checkerboard choice

In other work, in 1955, Dr. R. A. McConnell tested 393 subjects at the University of Pittsburgh and was unable to detect PK in over 170,000 dice throws. However, later analysis of his statistics did uncover the QD and decline effect observed by other researchers. McConnell's subjects consistently produced more hits in the first quarter of a run than in the last.

The next stage in Duke University's quest for scientific proof of PK came with the development of lateral placement tests. Instead of trying to influence which face of a dice would be uppermost, the placement PK experiments were designed to affect

where the dice would be when they came to rest. Researcher W. E. Cox conducted the first trials, using a checkerboard placed inside the bottom of a typewriter case. The squares on the board were numbered from one to six. Cox repeatedly threw 24 dice into the box, and subjects tried to will them to land on specific preselected squares. The trials produced what seemed to be positive PK results.

Selective fall

Cox went on to build a three-tier platform device in which the dice were pushed down a chute to the first level, then on down a corrugated runway to the next tier and finally bounced to the bottom, which was divided into squares marked A and B. Subjects were asked to try to influence the dice to land on either the A or B squares marked on the

---

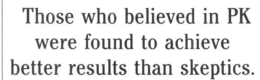

Those who believed in PK were found to achieve better results than skeptics.

---

lowest tier. Cox also used this experiment to test his theory that not all the dice would be influenced by PK. He believed that those affected would make it to the bottom and had a good chance of landing where the subject wanted them to be, and that others might be affected negatively and be trapped on the first or second levels. The accuracy of Cox's theory was difficult to judge, but Cox's subjects certainly produced scores that were well above what would be predicted by chance.

Swedish parapsychologist Haakon Forwald also experimented with placement PK. He used a platform and chute that led the falling dice onto a table top divided in two. In his tests Forwald endeavored to use PK to make the dice fall alternately

Princeton experiments

MECHANICAL ROLL

In 1979, Robert Jahn of Princeton University began studying PK, using highly sophisticated equipment. Volunteers were asked to "think high" or "think low" and influence a computer readout. Jahn's team detected small but consistent deviations from chance in 87 separate experiments.

Significant results have also been achieved by using a "random mechanical cascade." The machine has 9,000 black polystyrene balls that are allowed to roll down a slope, while subjects try to make more balls land on one side at the bottom.

A 1940's style dice board

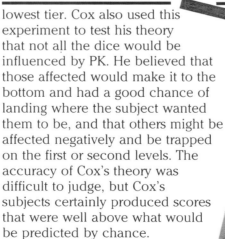

on each side of the dividing line. When these attempts produced successful results, Forwald went on to use dice of different weights and materials, such as wood, aluminum, steel, plastic, and paper, to see if PK was more effective with one than another.

Throwing six dice at a time, using three of one material and three of another, Forwald tried to direct his PK powers either at just the wooden dice or the steel ones. In all of these tests he scored above chance, showing that PK appeared to have no preference for the composition of the objects the mind was trying to influence.

A 17-year-old boy achieved especially high scores for both coin-throwing and hitting the target on a roulette wheel.

Forwald did discover, however, that there seemed to be a psychological factor that inhibited his results. When he tried to influence the dice to land first on the side of the table he had labeled A, and then on side B, he was successful. But if he reversed the procedure and began the test by trying to make the dice land on B first and then A, the results were no better than chance. Forwald visited Duke University in 1957 to demonstrate his experiments. The initial runs were not impressive, but he eventually succeeded in replicating his earlier results.

Coins and roulette

Many scientists have experimented with similar techniques for demonstrating PK in the laboratory. Some researchers have used dice while others have tried different equipment. In 1950, S. R. Binski, a graduate student at the University of Bonn, tested a 17-year-old boy named Kastor Seibel. The teenage boy reportedly achieved especially high scores for both coin-throwing and hitting the correct target number on a roulette wheel. Yet however persuasive some results appear

to be, attempts to replicate such work at other laboratories have not always been successful. It is possible, some critics suggest, that Dr. Rhine and other researchers did not use adequate controls in their experiments.

Answering the critics

Skeptics are also justifiably wary about the staggering odds against chance that appear to have been achieved. Researchers have tried to answer their critics by introducing new controls in experiments and submitting data for independent analysis. Such efforts to improve objectivity and accuracy have been useful and important.

Techniques for research on PK are now much more sophisticated than in the early days when Dr. Rhine on was on his knees throwing dice in the laboratory. The most important advance has been the use of special machines that make it possible to generate random events and numbers. Such devices help determine more accurately if test results really differ significantly from what might happen in any event — just by pure chance. Another improvement is that computers are registering test results directly — which makes conscious or unconscious deviation less likely.

CHILDISH INFLUENCE

Dr. Susan Blackmore, a psychologist at Bristol University, England, has been a longtime researcher into the paranormal. She used her baby Emily to test the theory that PK is possible even when a subject has no idea that the phenomenon might exist. Dr. Blackmore put baby Emily in front of a computer screen that showed either electronic snow and no sound, or a smiling face and a nursery rhyme tune. The frequency with which the face and tune came up was controlled by a Random Number Generator (RNG) — which is similar to a Random Event Generator.

Baby Emily

Smile preferred

Baby Emily liked the smiling face and tune, so naturally she wanted them to appear more often. Dr. Blackmore's theory was that if Emily sat in front of the computer and wanted to see the face and tune, she would be able to use PK to influence the RNG. Dr. Blackmore found that the face and tune did appear more often than would happen by chance.

Dr. Rhine in the 1940's
The Parapsychological Association published a report in 1990 that looked at 73 studies, involving over 2 million dice throws, published since the pioneering days at Duke. The association's report concluded that "there can be a genuine relationship between mental intention and the fall of dice — but, obviously, no one has total control to achieve success every time."

TAKING NO CHANCES

Human nature makes it difficult to choose in a truly random way, so researchers have sought electronic assistance to help generate genuinely unbiased selections.

"NOT ENOUGH CONTROLS!" "Open to manipulation!" When critics of tests into psychokinesis (PK) complained loudly that the whole field was lacking in scientific regulation, some parapsychologists turned to the respectability of physics and the world of subatomic particles for help.

Dr. Helmut Schmidt, a German-born physicist, began to explore this area in 1969 at the Boeing Laboratories in Seattle. Later, he spent some time with Dr. J. B. Rhine at the Institute of Parapsychology in North Carolina and then moved to the Mind Science Foundation in San Antonio. To assist him in his research Dr. Schmidt developed a machine that utilizes the fundamental randomness found in the decay of radioactive material and the energy it emits. He called the device a Random Event Generator (REG).

Dr. Schmidt using an REG
For tests of ESP, subjects tried to predict which lights would appear next. For tests of PK, subjects attempted to influence the order in which lights would illuminate.

An REG is essentially a kind of electronic coin-flipper, consisting of an electronic oscillator that moves rapidly back and forth between "heads" and "tails" positions. This oscillator is linked to decaying radioactive material, which is in turn linked to a Geiger counter. When a radioactive decay signal is detected by the Geiger counter, the oscillator stops at the position it happens to be in at the time. Since the decay signal is completely random, there are equal chances for the oscillator to stop at heads or tails.

Flash of inspiration

In order to use the REG for PK research, Dr. Schmidt hooked the machine to a board displaying a circle of nine bulbs, only one of which could be lit at a time. If the generator showed a positive heads signal, the next light in a clockwise direction would light. If a negative tails signal came up on the random generator, then the next light in a counter-clockwise direction would flash. Dr. Schmidt asked his subjects to concentrate on trying to make the bulbs light up one after another in a

clockwise direction. Dr. Schmidt reported that his early subjects performed more effectively than pure chance would allow. One subject, he said, was so good that there were 1-billion-to-1 odds against her producing the same result by pure chance. Another subject had a very low score. Dr. Schmidt asked the two subjects to perform 50 runs of 128 trials (a trial being the lighting of a bulb) over 10 days. There was a dramatic contrast in the results. Dr. Schmidt pointed out that the odds, as he calculated them, were more than 10 million to 1 against there being such a large difference between the scores of two individuals.

In a variation of his flashing lights test, Dr. Schmidt used sound instead of light. Subjects wore headphones and listened to clicks made randomly as electrons were emitted by an REG. Subjects tried to make more clicks sound in their right ears. Again, the results were reportedly significant, as the subjects were able to do this more often than would be expected by chance.

Dedicated research

Ray Hyman at the University of Oregon Department of Psychology is a well-known critic of parapsychology. However, he has supported the view that Dr. Schmidt's varied experiments using REG's provide an important scientific contribution. As Hyman commented: "Schmidt's work is the most challenging ever to confront critics such as myself. His approach makes many of the earlier criticisms of parapsychological research obsolete. He is dedicated to being as scientific as possible and is the most sophisticated parapsychologist that I have encountered. If there are flaws in his work, they are not common or obvious."

REG at work
People don't choose numbers in a totally random way. For example, if individuals are asked to select a number, a high proportion will choose seven. REG's provide a truly random choice.

Moving
Experiments

Certain people may have the power to move objects without employing physical contact. Some researchers acknowledge that these effects appear to be real, but they are mystified as to how they happen.

NINA KULAGINA, BORN IN LENINGRAD IN 1928, was one of the best-known psychokinetic (PK) subjects in the world. Her psychic abilities were first explored at the city's Institute of Brain Research in the 1960's. Tests were carried out on people who could distinguish colors by touch, and these "eyeless sight" investigations received widespread publicity at the time.

Kulagina had realized that she could detect the colors of embroidery threads without even looking at them. When she mentioned this to her doctor, he referred her to the institute. During tests into Kulagina's eyeless sight researchers noticed another unexpected effect — small objects near to her fingertips appeared to move. This discovery encouraged a broader study of her powers.

Reports from the institute team suggested that Kulagina could indeed move objects from a distance. "An aluminum pipe was moved three inches, and a container of matches was shifted over a similar distance. Aluminum pipes were moved both under a glass lid and without the lid. The committee at the present time cannot give an explanation of the observed phenomena of the transference of objects."

Variety of materials

In the late 1960's Western scientists became interested in Kulagina's powers when they saw some of her experiments on film. One of these experiments featured small objects apparently moving about on their own inside a transparent box.

Soviet scientists found that Kulagina's abilities could be

Magic touch
Kulagina first discovered her powers when she found that she could "see" colors with her hands and "read" text blindfolded.

> "The committee cannot give an explanation of the observed phenomena of the transference of objects."

Nina at work
Kulagina tended to lose weight during PK exhibitions and showed other signs of physical stress. Her pulse rate was about 132 during a session, compared with 86 when she was resting. Her heart rate also increased, sometimes rising to 240 beats a minute.

directed at a variety of materials, including metals, plastics, and fabrics. Items moved on a variety of surfaces, from glass to wooden tabletops covered with cloths.

Researchers claimed that when Kulagina was working with new objects, they always moved away from her, but that she might draw them to her with practice. She required greater energy to move objects far away than objects close at hand, and sometimes two or more items would move simultaneously, not necessarily in the same direction.

Kulagina seemed to be able to exert PK on living tissues as well. She reportedly changed the beating rate of a disembodied frog's heart and stopped it altogether after 12 minutes. A frog's heart usually goes on beating for about four hours after it is taken out of the body. Kulagina also appeared to revive aquarium fish that were thought to be dead. One fish that had been floating upside down and showed no signs of life suddenly turned over and began swimming after her efforts to revive it.

Another aspect of her powers was that she could put her hand on another person's arm and create a sensation of burning heat. Some people experienced real pain as a result of this contact, and burn marks appeared on their skin.

Magnetic personality

When Kulagina worked, she reported pain in her muscles, especially in her hands and feet. She also found it difficult to demonstrate her PK abilities in hot weather, and storms and high levels of humidity inhibited her activities. In addition, a strong magnetic field was detected around Kulagina's body during her demonstrations. Voltage potentials at the front and back of her scalp were reportedly 10 times higher than those of other people.

Rolling objects

While Kulagina was one of the most successful PK subjects ever studied, other people have shown similar powers. In the 1970's Alla Vinogradova reportedly produced impressive results in Moscow. She appeared to be able to roll objects weighing up to three ounces and could slide items weighing up to one ounce, all from a distance.

New Yorker Felicia Parise is another subject whose abilities were studied in experiments carried out in the 1970's. She seemed to operate under a great deal of stress, and never succeeded in moving items as forcefully, or with the same complexity of movement, as Kulagina. Researchers stated that Parise was able to move only small objects that

> ## Parise worked in an excited state in which she wanted to make the item move more than anything else in the world.

weighed very little. Nevertheless, items seemed to slide away from her.

Parise trembled and perspired profusely during PK sessions. Sometimes she precipitated movement quickly, and sometimes it took hours to achieve results. Her alleged PK ability seemed to be reduced if she were not concentrating at the right level. She spoke of working herself up to an excited state in which she wanted to make the item move more than anything else in the world.

ABRACADABRA

Felicia Parise watched with interest in 1971 when films of Nina Kulagina's PK abilities were shown at the Division of Parapsychology and Psychophysics at Maimonides Medical Center in New York. Parise was a good ESP subject and decided that she too could demonstrate PK. After weeks of practice concentrating on a small plastic bottle, Charles Honorton, director of research at the center, reported that she was finally able to move it. He said that she focused on the object, so that it was the only thing she was aware of, until it shifted in short bursts.

Parise was also tested at the Foundation for Research on the Nature of Man, where researchers found that her PK ability included being able to deflect a compass needle. Honorton reported that he suggested that Parise "zap" a compass while she was in his office. She was not in the mood for PK tests, she said, so she simply waved her arm in the direction of the compass and flippantly said "Abracadabra." Honorton said that the needle suddenly swung 90°.

THOUGHTOGRAPHY

Some exponents of PK believe that it is possible to bypass the conventional photographic process and to use the power of the mind to transfer images on to film.

THE PHENOMENON OF what is called thought-photography, or "thoughtography," has its roots in Japan. In 1910 Tomokichi Fukurai, a professor of psychology at Tokyo University, tested a woman, Mrs. Ikuko Nagao, who was known for her psychic powers. Mrs. Nagao agreed to undergo tests during which she would try to identify clairvoyantly an image imprinted on an undeveloped film plate. After the test Prof. Fukurai was surprised to discover that Mrs. Nagao had created a kind of image on another plate.

Prof. Fukurai then asked Mrs. Nagao to attempt to transfer images, usually Japanese characters or geometric figures, on to unexposed film plates. No camera was used and the plate was placed between two others. The woman successfully imprinted the middle plate with the specified image. The professor continued his experiments with other subjects, and published a book, *Clairvoyance and Thoughtography*, which detailed his apparently successful results. The controversy that followed the publication of this book, however, was so great that it prompted his resignation from the university.

Film revival

Thoughtography was revived in the 1960's when Dr. Jule Eisenbud, a Denver psychiatrist, began exploring the claims of Ted Serios, a Chicago hotel elevator operator. Serios stated that he could impose images on a Polaroid film by looking into the camera lens. He said that he had managed to produce pictures of people, buildings, and cars. Between 1964 and 1967, Serios worked with over three dozen scientifically trained observers. He produced more than 400 images on over 100 different themes.

During a session, Serios concentrated intensely, his eyes open and lips compressed. There was tension in his muscles. He consumed liquor and beer as he worked, and his heavy drinking seemed a part of the picture-producing phenomena.

In order to create his photographs Serios held a roll of black paper, which he called his gizmo, in his right hand and put it up to the lens of the camera. He then held up his left hand and brought it down in a sweeping motion as he excitedly shouted

"Now" or "Go." His shout was a signal for the experimenter to open the camera shutter.

Magician and skeptic James Randi has been highly critical of Serios's claims, insisting that he used his gizmo to distract researchers. The staff of *Popular Photography* magazine were also doubtful about the abilities of the hotel worker. The editors sent a magician and two photographers to investigate Serios, but he was unable to produce a thought-photograph for them. The journal subsequently published a debunking article on thoughtography.

Character analysis
"Thought-photographs" of Japanese characters were included in Prof. Fukurai's book Clairvoyance and Thoughtography.

Although some thought-photographs may have been produced by fraudulent means, other results remain a puzzle. The Russian psychic Nina Kulagina also seemed to be able to affect photosensitive material, but she produced only simple patterns, such as a cross or a letter. Kulagina underwent tests that involved wrapping unexposed 35mm film in an opaque cover around her head. When researchers examined the films on completion of the experiment, they found visible flashes on the film, suggesting the existence of some form of energy discharges.

Dorchagraph
Thoughtography apparently took place in the late-19th century, when certain psychics claimed to be able to transfer thought-held images on to film. The resulting pictures were known as dorchagraphs.

SORRAT map
In 1989 the Society for Research on Rapport and Telekinesis (SORRAT) produced this "thought" image that seems to show the earth as seen from space.

THE TURIN SHROUD

Although the Turin Shroud is a simple cloth made of linen, it continues to provoke worldwide speculation. The shroud features a lightly shaded Christ-like image, and believers claim that it is the very cloth that was used to cover Christ's body after the Crucifixion.

However, radiocarbon dating has shown that the fabric originates from the early 14th century. As a result, scientists say it could not have been Christ's shroud. But the mystery of how the image was made remains.

Hysterical reaction

In 1990 the *Journal of the Society for Psychical Research* put forward the theory of retro-thoughtography to explain the mystery of the shroud. The journal hypothesized that while the shroud was being used as an altar cloth in Lirey, France, in or about 1350, a group of worshippers who were emotionally aroused might have projected their hysteria toward the fabric. The theory suggests that without realizing it they may have created a retrographic portrait of the Saviour using the combined power of their minds.

Clock click
London's famous clock tower Big Ben appeared in this thought-photograph produced by Serios in Los Angeles.

Hotel snap
Ted Serios was aiming to show the Denver Hilton in this thought-photograph, but the result looks more like the Chicago Hilton.

Serios at work
Most of Ted Serios's thought-photographs were produced in frantic late-night sessions organized by psychiatrist Dr. Jule Eisenbud.

Familiar curves
The Capitol dome in Washington D.C. was another building that Serios managed to reproduce in one of his thought-photographs.

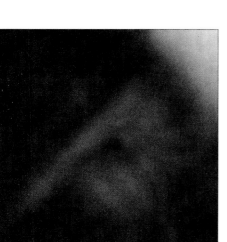

Prehistoric flashback
Serios's thought-photograph of a crouching prehistoric man is remarkably like a sculpted model to be found in the Field Museum of Natural History in Chicago.

TABLE-TURNING

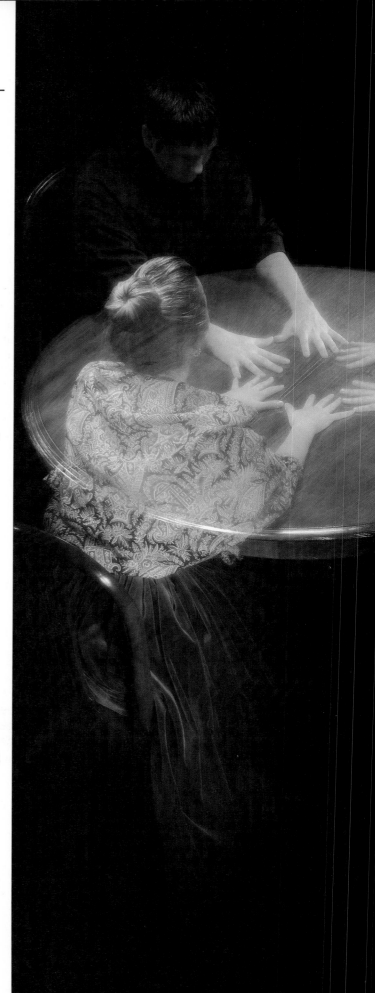

"I have no doubt that there are thousands of tables turning every night in London, so general is the excitement on the subject."
Writer and skeptic Sir David Brewster, 1853

ONE OF THE MOST REMARKABLE and widespread demonstrations of supposed psychokinesis — table-turning — enjoyed the peak of its popularity in the mid-1800's. English poet Elizabeth Barrett Browning, an enthusiast of things paranormal, commented on the table-turning craze she had witnessed in Paris in a letter to a friend, Mrs. Haworth. Browning declared that tables were speaking "alphabetically and intelligently," and she wondered whether anything similar was happening back in England.

In fact, table-turning seemed to be sweeping the Western world. In many countries people were sitting around tables, their fingertips resting lightly on the surface and touching their neighbors' hands. Sitters waited for the slightest tremor or movement from the table. Their patience was usually rewarded with rapping sounds that tapped out answers in a simple code. One rap meant "yes," two meant "uncertain," while three raps from the table meant "no."

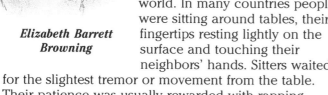

Elizabeth Barrett Browning

Alternatively, a sitter would recite the alphabet and the table would rap when the desired letter was mentioned. This process would be repeated in a laborious way until messages were spelled out. Sometimes sitters claimed that the table would start levitating, rocking from side to side, and even dancing about the room as they tried to keep up with it.

Some reports spoke of tables rising to such heights that those taking part in the experiment could talk to each other *under* the table, satisfying themselves that no one was cheating. And the phenomenon was not confined to tables — pianos, armchairs, and other items of furniture were also said to jump around.

Jumping piano

According to the reports of U.S. Army colonel Simon F. Kase, President Abraham Lincoln witnessed table-turning while attending a séance in the Washington home of a Mrs. Laurie and her daughter, Mrs. Miller.

Col. Kase claimed that as the daughter sat down at a piano and started to play, the front of the piano rose from the floor and began beating heavy thuds in time with the tune. Col. Kase asked if he could sit on the instrument to "verify to the world that it moved." And

he, a judge, and two soldiers who had accompanied Lincoln, sat on top of the piano, but it continued to move as before. "It was too rough riding; we got off while the instrument beat the time until the tune was played out," Kase solemnly reported.

Queen Victoria and Prince Albert indulged in table-turning at Osborne House on the Isle of Wight. They claimed positive results and decided that either magnetism or electricity had been responsible.

However, not everyone was impressed with the phenomenon. A committee of four doctors investigated table–turning and published their conclusions in the *Medical Times and Gazette,* June 11, 1853.

The doctors said that a table rotated only when those sitting around it expected it to, especially if the direction of rotation had been agreed upon by the sitters in advance. If the participants had not decided in what direction the table would move, nothing happened. The committee argued that the rotation was due to unconscious muscular action on the part of the sitters.

Muscular influence

Prompted by the enormous interest in table-turning in the mid-19th century, Michael Faraday, the English physicist, conducted a demonstration indicating that muscular action could be responsible for a table's movements. He placed several glass rods as thick as pencils between two small boards that were held together by two rubber bands. If pressure was applied to the upper board, it would slide over the lower one. A piece of paper was fastened to the boards to indicate the slightest movement of the upper board.

Every time there was movement, it was the top board that moved, indicating that pressure from the sitters' fingers was responsible. Faraday also pointed out that once the sitters knew the purpose of the paper indicator, no movement at all occurred.

In 1853, Prof. Robert Hare of the University of Pennsylvania decided to

POWER AT OUR FINGERTIPS

Count Agenor de Gasparin held table-turning séances in his Swiss home in the early 1850's. About 12 people would sit around the table with their hands palm down and fingers outstretched. The team found that the table moved within about five minutes.

Weighty matters

During one sitting, a 190-pound man sat on the table as it rose. Gasparin thought the psychology of the sitters was very important. He wrote: "When a person is in a state of nervous tension, he or she becomes positively unfit to act upon the table. It must be handled cheerfully, lightly, deftly, with confidence and authority, but without passion."

Gasparin concluded that the table movements were produced by a "psychic fluid" within people. He believed that the PK effect was produced entirely by the sitters and not by outside spirits.

Gasparin

A Gasparin séance

Kathleen Goligher

AN UPLIFTING FAMILY

In 1914, Dr. W. J. Crawford of Queen's College in Belfast, Northern Ireland, began a six-year research project on the Goligher family, particularly 18-year-old daughter Kate. The spiritualist Golighers sat around a table and sang until the table moved or emitted raps.

Dr. Crawford believed that the force behind the Golighers' PK effect traveled like a beam from Kathleen's body to the floor and then projected upward toward the table.

Cover up

The Society for Psychical Research sent researcher Fournier d'Albe to make an independent report on the Golighers. He produced a more negative conclusion. Albe thought the Golighers sang to cover up the noises they made while faking the levitations.

Kathleen moves a table

expose the "gross delusion" of spiritualism by carrying out a number of laboratory experiments on table-turning, which attempted to prove that sitters were moving tables manually. Yet after much work, Prof. Hare was reportedly unable to come up with a scientific explanation for the phenomenon, and, so the story goes, was converted to spiritualism.

In June 1973, spiritualists Rev. Stainton Moses and Sgt. Cox reported on their own spontaneous table-turning session, which took place

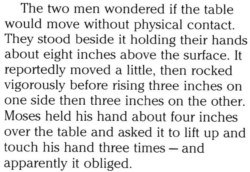

K. J. Batcheldor

at Cox's London house. While Cox opened letters, Moses sat reading *The Times*. For half an hour the two men heard loud rappings coming from a table next to Rev. Moses. While still holding his newspaper with both hands, Moses rested his arm on the table, which began to sway and then move forward.

The two men wondered if the table would move without physical contact. They stood beside it holding their hands about eight inches above the surface. It reportedly moved a little, then rocked vigorously before rising three inches on one side then three inches on the other. Moses held his hand about four inches over the table and asked it to lift up and touch his hand three times — and apparently it obliged.

An entertaining turn

Table-turning enjoyed its heyday in the days before radio and television, when it brought entertainment and mystery into the lives of people in many countries. But spelling out messages in this way was very tedious and it was a matter of time before the activity was replaced by new vogues, such as the ouija board. For researchers, however, the demonstration

of PK at work through table-turning continued to be worthy of study.

British researcher Kenneth J. Batcheldor, a former clinical psychologist for a group of Devon hospitals, studied levitation phenomena for over 20 years. During this time he claimed that a variety of table movements and raps were produced at his group's regular meetings and some of these effects are reportedly recorded on videotape. In 1966 he published several reports based on his studies.

Batcheldor concluded that it was essential for subjects to believe in the possibility of PK for it to occur. He said that "doubtful thoughts create only doubtful phenomenon, or maybe none at all." Batcheldor acknowledged that table movements at the start of a session might well be due to unconscious muscular activity — but he thought these encouraged later genuine movements by mysterious or unexplained forces.

> ## The table moved a little, then rocked vigorously before rising three inches on one side then three inches on the other.

Up, up, and away
A table appears to levitate during Batcheldor's PK experiments.

Detecting fraud
A Victorian lady demonstrates one of Prof. Hare's contraptions for determining if people were moving tables manually rather than spiritually.

Mini-Labs

You do not need a full-scale laboratory to test for PK. All that is really required is a see-through container fitted with a secure, lockable base. Put a selection of objects inside, secure the locks, and then wait for something out of the ordinary to happen.

EXPERIMENTS HAVE SUGGESTED that a wide variety of PK phenomena can be encouraged inside a specially constructed, locked container when individuals with alleged psychic powers are present. Such a container is called a Cox's mini-lab, after PK specialist W. E. Cox, who worked at Dr. J. B. Rhine's Institute for Parapsychology, based at Duke University in North Carolina.

The work first began in 1961 when John G. Neihardt, a professor of English literature, founded a group of experimenters who called themselves the Society for Research on Rapport and Telekinesis, or SORRAT. Meeting every Friday evening at Neihardt's home in Rolla, Missouri, the members had very little success at first. But after a while they began to report impressive occurrences of levitation and rapping. Later, when Neihardt informed Dr. Rhine of these activities, Rhine despatched Cox to help SORRAT with their research by imposing various controls on their experiments. As well as being an experienced psychic researcher, Cox was also a talented amateur magician, and therefore ideally suited to detecting fraud. The most important control he set up was his mini-lab, fitted out with various tamperproof devices so that it could be left unattended for long periods of time. Prof. Neihardt's death in 1973 caused the group to lose its focus for a while, but research eventually began again at the home of Dr. J. T. Richards, SORRAT's archivist, and soon the team was working with renewed vigor.

By 1977, the group was producing seemingly extraordinary results: Besides the mini-lab phenomena, a tray was reported to have levitated in the air for three minutes; a table apparently danced in the backyard before it rose 13 feet, floated horizontally, then slowly descended; books appeared to be taken off shelves by invisible hands. Fired with enthusiasm by these alleged happenings, Cox decided to devote himself full-time to SORRAT research. In terms of theory, Cox was convinced that the subconscious mind was responsible for PK activity, while other group members thought that it might be caused by spirits.

In 1979, cameras were connected to the mini-lab to record some of the dramatic events described. These reportedly included the movement of objects inside the box, the sudden appearance and disappearance of a variety of items, and the strange linking and unlinking of leather rings.

Filmed evidence
W. E. Cox with a locked, sealed mini-lab box. Any movement inside the box set off an automatic device that could film spontaneous PK events.

Loopy loops
In 1987, W. E. Cox put unlinked solid leather rings in a plastic envelope. These rings were said to link and then unlink again.

Mystery face
In a 1985 experiment, researchers claimed that a face was drawn on a Ping-Pong ball while it was inside a sealed glass jar.

Sealed spoon
Putting objects in sealed glass containers is a way of trying to eliminate fraud from experiments.

Recording PK
This mini-lab, built in 1979, had electrical connections for lights and cameras to record movements.

Ghost writer
Tony Cornell of the Cambridge Society for Psychical Research in England doubts the claims of SORRAT and has shown how the results could be faked. If a film is made frame-by-frame, moving a pencil slightly each time, the viewer might be led to believe that the pencil was writing on its own.

RAISED EXPECTATIONS

Magicians employ trickery to levitate subjects, but is it possible to use spiritual or mental powers to defy the laws of gravity?

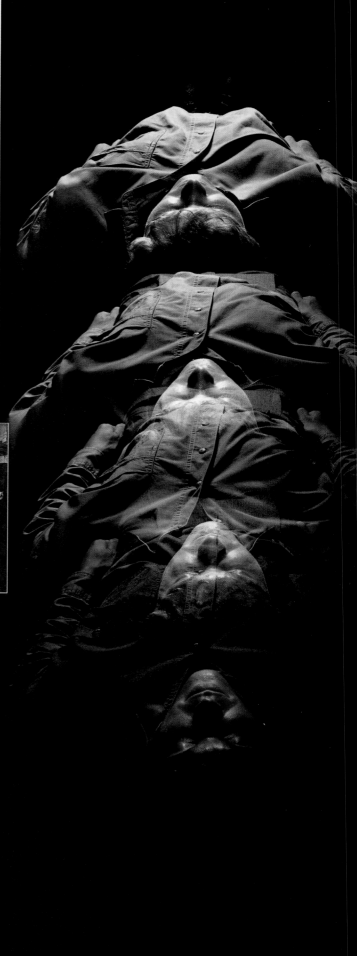

LEVITATION MEANS "RISING OR LIFTING a person by some supernatural means." Yet magicians state that there is nothing supernatural about the remarkable levitations that they include in their performances, even if they won't reveal their methods. However, the Society for Psychical Research has recorded numerous reports of subjects who have apparently raised either themselves, other people, or inanimate objects, without the use of trickery. And in some instances levitators seemed to have no control over their loss of contact with the ground.

In the 1920's a French explorer, Madame Alexandra David-Neel, came upon a man in Tibet weighted down with heavy chains. A companion explained that the man's mystical training had made his body so light that he would float away if the chains were not there to hold him down.

Joseph of Cupertino (1603–63)

This is not an isolated case. A 17th-century Italian saint, Joseph of Cupertino, was said to be embarrassed by his untimely levitations. He would suddenly cry out and find himself up in the air. At Mass one Sunday, he flew onto the altar and into the candles, suffering severe burns, and had to stay away from church services as a result. Despite this restriction his levitations continued. Apparently Joseph was not the only saint to have experienced levitation. In 1875, the British scientist Sir William Crookes published a list of "Forty Levitated Persons, Canonized or Beatified" in *The Quarterly Journal of Science*.

Send-up
Punch *magazine published this satirical cartoon on levitation in 1863.*

MENTALLY UPLIFTING

India has been a world center for levitation for centuries. The Transcendental Meditation (TM) movement that originated there tells followers that they may rise as a result of a type of breath control known as *pranayama*. Students must sit in a cross-legged position and practice systematic deep relaxation along with a cycle of inhalation, breath retention, and exhalation. Although followers may not leave the ground, this technique can generate a mentally uplifted state.

Believers think that collective mind power may be stronger than that of an individual, and that levitation can be produced by harnessing the collective power of a group of believers.

Helping hands

In order to attempt to use collective mind power to carry out a levitation, four people need to gather round the subject, who sits on a chair. The four people put their hands over, but do not press on, the subject's head so that no hands are touching. The levitators then concentrate deeply for 15 seconds. On the count of 15 they quickly put their fingers under the person in the chair. According to believers, even a heavy person will float into the air using this technique.

Ancient levitators
The outline of pictures like this white horse in Uffington, Oxfordshire, England, needs to be seen from the air to be fully appreciated. Believers in levitation have speculated that the ancient designers of such works used levitation in order to view their creations from above.

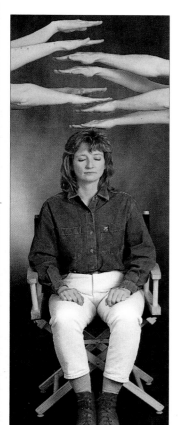

On the move?
Levitators put their fingers under armpits and knees and attempt to raise the subject using their collective mind power.

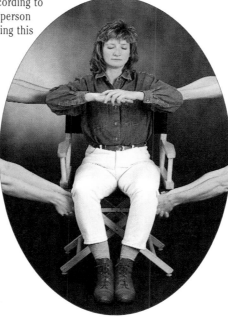

Under pressure
Levitators place their hands over the subject's head and concentrate for 15 seconds.

St. Teresa of Ávila
St. Teresa of Ávila was a 16th-century saint who was said to levitate. She commented that whenever she tried to resist, it was as if "a great force beneath my feet lifted me up." She begged other sisters to hold her down when she felt an attack of weightlessness approaching.

Mystery balance
Magicians are able to produce spectacular levitation effects. Subjects float miraculously with no obvious means of support.

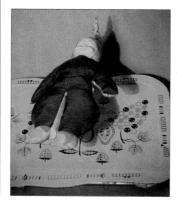

SORRAT dolls
The Missouri-based Society for Research on Rapport and Telekinesis (SORRAT) reportedly levitated dolls as part of its experimental research.

THE GELLER CONTROVERSY

Uri Geller is well-known as the man who bends metal and reads minds. But is he demonstrating paranormal ability — or simply revealing the skills of a very talented magician? Whatever his methods, Geller has sparked one of the great psychic debates of the 20th century.

EARLY DAYS

In his autobiography, *My Story,* Geller describes an incident that he says happened in 1949, when he was three years old. He writes that while playing in a garden near his Tel-Aviv home: "Suddenly there was a very loud, high-pitched ringing. Something made me look up at the sky. There was a silvery mass of light which came down lower, very close to me. There was a sharp pain in my forehead and I was knocked out. When I woke I rushed home and told my mother. She was angry and worried. Deep down, I knew that something important had happened."

Developing powers

Geller claims that after this incident, he started to develop unusual abilities. For example, when his mother returned from a card-playing session with friends, he says he was able to say exactly how much she had won or lost. By the age of seven, he claims the hands of his watch sometimes bent and jumped ahead. At the age of eight, a spoon broke in his hand as he was eating soup. One day at the zoo, a feeling of terror supposedly came over him and he insisted on leaving. It was only after he had left that alarm bells signaled that a lion had escaped from its cage.

GELLERMANIA CAPTURED the imagination of people all over the world in the 1970's, after the young Israeli began appearing on television talk shows. In particular, Uri Geller's performance on the British *David Dimbleby Talk-in*, on November 23, 1973, put him firmly on the road to fame and fortune.

Geller apparently managed to "see" a secret drawing that had been sealed in an envelope. He rubbed two broken watches, causing them to start, and also bent a metal fork which was being held securely in the hand of the TV program's host. Dozens of viewers phoned in to report that their own cutlery had bent mysteriously.

If the effects had been achieved by a self-confessed magician, no one would have thought twice about them. But Geller insisted that his demonstration involved the use of psychic powers. The resultant

"One hundred years ago we'd have burned Uri Geller at the stake. Now we put him on the Johnny Carson show."

media attention meant that Geller was in great demand to display his psychic wares around the world. As James Fadiman of Stanford University said: "One hundred years ago we'd have burned Uri Geller at the stake. Now we put him on the Johnny Carson show."

Yet by the early 1990's, after two decades of controversy, things had changed. Geller, his wife, and their two children had settled in a quiet English village. High iron gates protect the privacy of their estate. Crystals adorn the white mansion, along with antique Japanese robes and other souvenirs of Geller's travels. He has become a multimillionaire entrepreneur.

Along the way, phenomena linked with Geller have been supported as remarkable by some scientists — and just as emphatically dubbed sleight of hand by others. And thus, in a very real sense Geller, and the nature of his abilities, remain as controversial as ever.

A MATTER OF OPINION

Uri Geller provokes strong responses from both his critics and his devotees:

◆ "Every magic shop sells manuscripts on how to do the key-bending trick. The kids vie with one another for a new way to 'do a Geller.'"
James Randi, *The Magic of Uri Geller*

◆ "We are told by Stanford Research Institute that some thirty thousand feet of movie film about the Geller experiments was prepared. We are offered only that which was released by Targ and Puthoff as the best of their data —and most of what is shown is admittedly not done under proper control."
James Randi, *Flim-Flam*

◆ "Every Geller event that I could investigate in detail had a normal explanation that was more probable than a paranormal one."
Dr. Joseph Hanlon, *New Scientist*, October 17, 1974

◆ "Dr. Hanlon's approach was identical to Randi's, looking at how Geller could have cheated. The argument sounds convincing — but it is like trying to prove that there is no life on earth by arguing that the chances are a million to one against it. The things Geller does seem to contradict our everyday experience of the world. But then, the properties of X-rays and radioactivity also contradict our experience of the everyday world, yet they have become the basis of a new type of physics — quantum mechanics."
Colin Wilson, *The Geller Phenomenon*

◆ "The powers may be hidden in all of us but some people have a much higher level of them than others....The more I think of it, the more I see how small we all are. How much we don't know, how much more there is to know."
Uri Geller, *My Story*

A TESTING TIME

Geller has been tested extensively in laboratories, with some impressive results. However, many of the experiments are still the subject of intense debate.

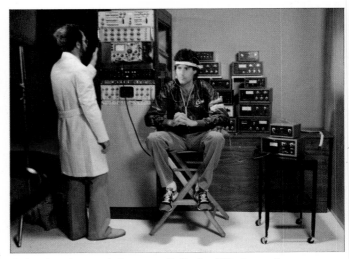
Scientists have tried to test Geller's skills in various ways

THE FIRST MAJOR SCIENTIFIC experiments with Uri Geller were carried out in 1972 by Russell Targ and Harold Puthoff at the Stanford Research Institute (SRI). Targ and Puthoff were primarily interested in the possibility that the Israeli could be clairvoyant and telepathic. Typical tests had Geller selecting which of a number of cans contained an object, and indicating what face was uppermost on dice in a closed metal box. Geller performed well, but his scores were far from perfect.

In October 1974 a report on the Geller experiments carried out at SRI was published in the English scientific journal *Nature*. The magazine asked three independent referees to evaluate the report, and they concluded that not enough safeguards had been taken during the experiments. However, in its preface to the article, *Nature* said that whatever the shortcomings of the research, publishing the report was "serving notice on the community that there is something worthy of their attention and scrutiny."

Altered structure

Experiments conducted by other researchers tested Geller's apparent ability in another area of ESP, namely the ability to influence matter with the mind, which is known as psychokinesis (PK). In 1973 Eldon Byrd, physicist at the Naval Surface Weapons Center in Silver Spring, Maryland, reported: "Geller altered the lattice structure of a metal alloy in a way that cannot be duplicated. There is no present scientific explanation as to how he did this."

Geller was also tested by William Cox at the Institute of Parapsychology in Durham, North Carolina. Cox testified that Geller simply stroked a very thick blank key, making it curl upward by 12 degrees in less than a

> **Geller simply stroked a thick blank key, making it curl upward by 12 degrees in less than a minute**

minute. Cox kept his own finger on the key while the experiment was taking place and was unable to explain how or why it had been bent.

In 1974 Prof. John Hasted, head of the physics department at Birkbeck College, University of London, became interested in Geller. He ran a number of experiments and reported that Geller had caused a Geiger counter to malfunction wildly. Prof. Hasted also studied children who claimed to possess similar PK abilities, and although there was no proof that Geller was cheating, the same cannot be said for all others claiming similar psychic gifts. In 1975 at the University of Bath, England, some children said to be "mini-Gellers" were caught trying to physically bend spoons. The children thought they were unobserved, but scientists in another room were watching them through a one-way mirror.

Sudden halt

Geller's diverse talents have been tested in numerous ways by scientists and researchers all over the world. In 1985, editors at *Computerworld* magazine reported seeing a videotape of Geller "applying his powers to microelectronics with some surprising results." The video showed tests carried out the previous year by scientists at Tokai University in Tokyo. They had asked Geller to try and halt a computer graphics system that was displaying continuous images. Nothing happened on the first day or for over three hours on the second day, until Geller suddenly shouted "Stop" and completely halted the image. When the astonished scientists ran the computer tape over and over again, they reported that it always stopped at the same point.

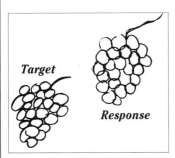
Target / **Response**

Seeing double
Geller claims to have had a high success rate when attempting to identify a drawn image which has been placed in a sealed envelope. At SRI he duplicated the target image of a bunch of grapes, and his drawing even included the same number of grapes as the original.

To his credit, Geller has continually obliged supporters and critics alike by participating in a wide range of laboratory experiments. In some cases, the extraordinary events that happened before and after the experiments have become part of the Geller legend.

One such incident apparently occurred in August, 1972, when Gerald Feinberg, a Columbia University physicist, was lunching with Geller, parapsychologist Dr. Andrija Puharich, and astronaut Ed Mitchell and his secretary. Geller asked the secretary to take off her gold ring and hold it in her fist. He then waved his hand over hers. Feinberg described what he saw: "She opened her hand and the ring appeared with a crack in it, as if it had been cut through with some kind of extremely sharp instrument.

Bizarre effects

"Initially there was a very small space, probably only a fraction of an inch. Geller then took the ring, putting it down on a table. Over a few hours, the ring twisted and went gradually into the shape of an S."

Reports of incidents of this kind helped spread Geller's fame, and accounts of his alleged abilities appeared in books, magazines, and newspapers all over the world. As Geller's notoriety increased, his seemingly inexplicable feats began to occur on an infinitely grander scale — spoons and watches were replaced by ocean liners and huge buildings. For example, in the mid-1970's, Geller was traveling on the liner *Renaissance* between Spain and Italy. Musicians from the ship's orchestra dared him to try and stop the ship, and to their amazement the vessel soon slowed down and then lost all power. The cause of the trouble was found to be a crimped fuel line.

> ## "Geller works in a high state of excitement... making it difficult to keep your mind on what is happening."

Geller in front of Big Ben

Had Geller's powers bent the line, or was the breakdown just a lucky malfunction?

The same question applies to an incident that took place on December 17, 1989, when London's landmark timepiece Big Ben tick-tocked to a halt. Geller claimed responsibility for the breakdown, explaining that he was experimenting in order to make the huge clock stop at midnight on New Year's Eve at the request of an American games firm. Geller has a fax from the company dated December 16 confirming the deal.

Quite clearly Geller has never been 100 percent successful — or even close to it — in laboratories, on stage, or in other efforts. Yet despite his failures, some scientists became convinced that his work merited further study.

Mixed opinions

For example, Dr. Friedbert Karger, of the Max Planck Institute of Plasma Physics, Munich, has said: "The powers of this man are a phenomenon which theoretical physics cannot yet explain." While some scientists have been impressed, others have continued to express their doubts.

Prof. David Bohm was present in 1974 at tests performed with Geller at London University. Prof. Bohm admitted there was an element of confusion during the tests: "Geller works in a high state of excitement which communicates to experimenters, making it difficult to keep your mind on what is happening."

Desire to believe

Physicist Dr. Joseph Hanlon, who was selected by the British journal *New Scientist* to investigate Geller, concluded that the phenomenon was strongly linked to the Israeli's personality: "He exudes sincerity, which makes people really want to believe in him."

Trance discoveries
Dr. Andrija Puharich, an American physician, parapsychologist, and hypnotist, was the first scientist to look into Geller's background in any depth. Dr. Puharich's book Uri *was one of many publications to investigate Geller's powers.*

Moon message
In 1971 Ed Mitchell became the sixth U.S. astronaut to walk on the moon. On that mission Mitchell tried an experiment in telepathy by attempting to communicate a series of numbers to friends on earth. Mitchell met Geller in 1972 and encouraged scientific testing of the Israeli.

♦ PAGE 132

SKEPTICS VS. BELIEVERS

The Geller controversy highlights the views of people who have wider doubts about the psychic world in general. Skeptics insist that claimants of paranormal powers must be either deluding themselves or deliberately trying to fool others.

IN MAY 1976 A GROUP of 25 people — including scientists, authors, and magician James Randi — met at a humanist symposium in Buffalo, New York. Randi explained their reason for getting together: "We were determined to do something about the unfounded claims of miracles and magical powers that were being supported by a few scientists and were alleged to be real scientific discoveries." As a result of the symposium, the Committee for the Scientific Investigation of Claims of the Paranormal (CSICOP) was formed.

In-depth investigation

The purpose of the committee was to establish a network of people who wanted to investigate the paranormal in depth by commissioning and publishing objective research. James Randi has emphasized that CSICOP does not deny that the paranormal may exist. As he has said: "I cannot prove that these powers do not exist; I can only show that the evidence for them does not hold up under examination."

Randi quite openly admits to trickery in his own performances. He has said: "I'm a charlatan, a liar, a thief, and a fake altogether. There's no question of it, but I'm an actor playing a part, and I do it for purposes of entertainment."

> **"Deliberately or accidentally, Geller manipulates the experiments to a degree of chaos where he feels comfortable and we feel uncomfortable."**

> **"If I were a professional magician, I would practice to the point where I would never fail...."**
> **Uri Geller**

Those who claim to perform amazing feats without sleight of hand find the magician a relentless opponent. Randi agrees that his own ability to duplicate psychic feats does not prove that psychics necessarily use similar techniques. But he says: "What it does show is that it is more rational to suspect trickery than to adopt the preposterous alternative."

Lack of control

The magician has criticized early experiments with Geller at the Stanford Research Institute (SRI) by physicists Harold Puthoff and Russell Targ. The laxity of controls has also been criticized by others, but Puthoff and Targ insist that: "In every instance Randi, in his efforts to fault the SRI experiments, hypothesized the existence of a loophole condition that did not exist." However, in *New Scientist*, October 17, 1974, Targ said: "Deliberately or accidentally, Geller manipulates the experiments to a degree of chaos where he feels comfortable and we feel uncomfortable."

Surely intelligent scientists steeped in the rigors of objective laboratory testing would not be easily misled into thinking an event was paranormal when it was not. The question has been raised by Martin Gardner, a journalist for *Scientific American*, an amateur magician, and also a leading member of CSICOP. Gardner insists that scientists, with their special perspective, are in fact

New direction
Geller claims to be able to influence the movements of a compass needle by using his psychic powers, but James Randi interprets the phenomenon in a more straightforward way:
"Geller is shown waving his hands about over a simple compass. We are assured that his hands have been carefully examined. The compass needle deflects but it moves only when his head approaches the device." Randi thinks Geller must have had a magnet in his mouth, but no such device has ever been found.

the easiest people in the world to fool. As he pointed out in *Technology Review*: "The thinking of a scientist is rational, based on a lifetime of experience with the rational world. But the methods of magic are irrational and totally outside a scientist's experience."

In the early 1980's Randi decided to demonstrate what he felt was the laxity of control methods used in research into the paranormal. To do this, he devised a hoax called Project Alpha. Two magicians, Stephen Shaw, age 18, and Michael Edwards, age 17, were planted as supposedly psychic subjects in the McDonnell Laboratory for Psychical Research at Washington University in St. Louis. The young men performed such feats as bending metal by stroking it and moving the hands of a watch. Parapsychologists thought they might be watching demonstrations of PK until Randi revealed the fraud.

Mystery, not magic
Randi does not speak for all magicians. There are a number who do not think Uri Geller is a conjurer. Arthur Zorka, a member of the Society of American Magicians, has said: "There is no way, based on my knowledge as a magician, that any method of trickery could have been used to produce the effects under the conditions to which Geller was subjected."

In *My Story*, published in 1975, Geller wrote: "Magicians can do some of the things I do and make them look real. When they perform on a stage under their own prescribed conditions, they never fail. I readily admit that I sometimes fail, and it's rather embarrassing when I do. If I were a professional magician, I would practice to the point where I would never fail either."

> "There is no way, based on my knowledge as a magician, that any method of trickery could have been used to produce the effects under the conditions to which Geller was subjected."

Yet Geller's failures also encourage his critics. Randi says that when experimental controls on Geller are strict, nothing paranormal takes place. Talk show host Johnny Carson followed the detailed advice of James Randi when Geller was scheduled to appear on the NBC *Tonight* show in August 1973. Under Randi's instruction, strict controls were in operation, and Randi insisted that nothing psychic happened during the broadcast, thus proving that Geller's "stunts" are possible only when controls are lax. In reply Geller says that a spoon did bend and that he had only limited success because he was nervous and he did not have enough time on the show.

Supporting players
Geller believes that he tends to perform badly if an audience or researchers are hostile towards him. He thinks the presence and attitude of others concerning his work is important, if not vital, to his success. As he has said, "I have never been able to bend an object unless there are at least one or two other people in the room."

Whether or not Randi and other skeptics are correct in their conclusions, the opinions of doubters have given support to the demand for ever tighter controls on experiments. In its 1974 preface to the SRI report, *Nature* magazine raised the question of "whether science has yet developed the competence to confront claims of the paranormal," and urged more care and far greater controls in experiments related to any category of psychic phenomena.

Fooling the experts
James Randi and fellow conspirators Stephen Shaw and Michael Edwards revealed their Project Alpha hoax at a press conference in 1983.

> "I'm a charlatan, a liar, a thief, and a fake...but I'm an actor playing a part, and I do it for purposes of entertainment."
> **James Randi**

Aerial prospecting

REMOTE SENSING

Geller says that remote sensing for minerals requires intense concentration and is very tiring. He studies maps for hours so that he will recognize main features when he flies over the area later. "Eventually I find myself zeroing in on certain regions which I mark in pencil. I check these over again for days or even weeks to make sure that my impressions stay the same."

Costly search

Once Geller has studied the land from the air he walks across the territory to locate spots more precisely. Geller maintains that companies pay him a great deal of money for his advice: "Digging up hundreds of square miles of jungle can take millions of man-hours and tens or hundreds of millions of dollars. It is not surprising that people are prepared to pay me quite a lot of money for telling them where to start digging, or where not to dig."

Since his early days of showtime and spectacle, Geller has been steadily broadening the scope of his activities. In the 1980's, he became a business consultant for companies requiring special advice. By the early 1990's, he had written four books — a novel about a psychic superman caught up in the cold war, two volumes of autobiography, and a book encouraging people to develop their own extrasensory abilities. He has also sponsored a variety of products — from jewelery and games, to cosmetics made without animal testing. Geller's strong interest in health (he is a vegetarian) and the environment has led him to provide financial support for related projects, including the production of wind turbines. Geller's 1990 appearance on a Russian television program resulted in 45,000 letters asking for help with health problems. But he said then that he did not feel ready to become more involved with healing.

Valuable resources

The main source of Geller's wealth has been his involvement in the search for minerals. Geller says that he is able to pinpoint where reserves of gold, oil, coal, or other similar resources are located. The Israeli was initially encouraged to develop this skill in the early 1970's, by Sir Val Duncan, the chairman of Rio Tinto Zinc. Duncan tested Geller by burying samples of metal somewhere on the island of Majorca, in the Mediterranean. According to Duncan, Geller successfully located the hidden metal.

In 1973 Geller was further encouraged to use his powers for mineral location when he met Clive Menell, chairman of Anglo-vaal, a mining company, while touring in South Africa. Menell invited Geller to his office, where he spread out a large map on a table. Menell then asked Geller to look at the map and suggest which particular area might have the best coal deposits.

Geller takes up the story: "I spread out my hands and moved them around

in the air above the map until I felt that magnetic sensation on one of my palms. I then scanned the area underneath with a fingertip and pointed to one very specific location." In 1980 *Newsweek* revealed that miners had discovered large deposits of coal in the area.

In May 1987 an article appeared in the magazine *International Mining* suggesting that the mining industry should take more notice of Geller's achievements and concluding: "It seems certain that his powers merit serious trial in exploration."

Complementary powers

As a result of Geller's successes working for various oil companies during the previous 10 years, Uri Geller Associates (UGA) was formed in the late 1980's. UGA combines the expert knowledge of a team of mining engineers and geologists with Geller's apparent talents to locate oilfields and mineral deposits. Geller says that his powers are meant to complement more conventional methods and are not a substitute for them.

> ## "I spread out my hands and moved them in the air above the map until I felt that magnetic sensation."

UGA charges large consultancy fees to companies that make use of Geller's advice, without giving any guarantee of results. Geller admits that he is not always right, but he claims that his techniques are more successful than the conventional methods used to locate

Group effort
Geller combines his skills with those of mining engineers prior to a UGA exploration project.

minerals. At the request of the companies he works for, Geller generally does not reveal their names. Most companies think that they might be ridiculed if their unusual associations with Geller were made public. As he says: "They would have to explain to their boards why I am employed and would find that embarrassing."

Geller working underwater

High-security meetings

Geller has revealed that his ever-widening range of clients has moved beyond the realm of big business to involvement with national governments. He claims that much of this non-company work is confidential and that therefore there is no public record of what has taken place. However, there

> ## "They would have to explain to their boards why I am employed and would find that embarrassing."

are some indications that certain high-powered meetings may have occurred.

For example, in May 1987, *Newsweek* reported a high-security meeting that took place in late April 1987 between 40 U.S. government officials (including top members of Congress, the CIA, Pentagon and Defense Department aides) and Geller. Across the Atlantic the British *Sunday Times* picked up the story and published a front page report on May 3, 1987, which carried the headline "Did Uri bend the will of Gorbachev?" The article suggested that the U.S. government may have employed Geller to beam "peace messages" into the minds of Soviet negotiators at the Geneva arms talks that were taking place that year.

Understandably, most politicians are as cautious as businessmen about being involved in employing the skills of a

psychic. But in 1987 Claiborne Pell, a five-term U.S. Senator and chairman of the Foreign Relations Committee, admitted his interest in Geller and stated that if psychic powers exist, they should be utilized for good. Geller himself shares this concern, believing that such powers could be put to harmful use in warfare: "What I want to use my gift for most is to put a desire for peace into the minds of those responsible for making global policy."

Safe ambiguity

What is the reality of Uri Geller's skill? Is he magician, psychic — or a combination of both? Geller himself says that we all have psychic powers within us waiting to be developed and that some day these will be understood.

One aspect that further fuels the controversy is that Geller encourages ambiguity about himself with such comments as: "No one knows if I am real or not." Geller has also stated that he thinks he is probably safer if people do not believe he is psychic. As he has said: "Whoever controls people with such powers has an incredible weapon."

A SATISFIED CUSTOMER

Peter Sterling is chairman of Zanex, an Australian minerals and exploration company. He is one businessman who is prepared to confirm that Geller has worked for his company.

In 1983 Sterling flew Geller to the Solomon Islands to help pinpoint gold deposits. Sterling says: "We sent Uri some topographic maps and he rang us back and said, 'You should be looking for diamonds on Malaita.' No one had thought of looking for diamonds on that island. We were skeptical, but he insisted."

Geller insisted even more strongly when he was flown over the islands. Soil samples were then taken and analyzed at the University of Melbourne. The report indicated that the sample showed "a high prospectivity for diamond-bearing host rocks." Sterling said he was pleased with his investment in Geller, but confirms that it hasn't been easy explaining such an unconventional involvement to his board and shareholders.

Uri Geller at a Zanex site in the Solomon Islands

POLTERGEIST!

Poltergeist activity, whatever its cause may be, can devastate a household. Strange and inexplicable noises may keep family members awake, powerful jets of water may suddenly spurt from walls, and items of furniture burst into flames.

WEIRD HAPPENINGS

The two most common poltergiest occurrences are sounds (raps, thuds, crashes) and objects moving of their own accord. There are other effects that have reportedly taken place, such as inundations of water, outbreaks of fire, electrical equipment malfunctioning, musical instruments playing mysteriously, clothes tearing, and objects arranging themselves into patterns. There never appears to be an obvious explanation for the strange goings-on, but they often seem to focus around one individual.

Airborne animals

In 1851 a French curé and his servant claimed to have seen furniture and animals flying around the rectory in Cideville, France. They believed that the extraordinary incident was the work of a poltergeist.

THE WORD POLTERGEIST comes from the German, and simply means a noisy spirit. However, the range of phenomena associated with poltergeist activity reaches far beyond noise. After years of extensive research, parapsychologists have concluded that poltergeist events, such as strange noises, floods without a source, spontaneous fires, moving objects, and bombardments with stones, may be caused involuntarily by the people who become the focus of activity. Some parapsychologists believe that without the individual even realizing it, his or her mind may give vent to repressed anger or frustrations in some inexplicable way. For that reason, researchers often do not talk about poltergeists as if they were some outside being, but rather use the term recurrent spontaneous psychokinesis (RSPK) to describe the phenomenon.

Lonely child

The effects of poltergeist activity on a household can be very disturbing — as illustrated by the experiences of the Campbell family in the the small town of Sauchie in Scotland. The Campbells' case was recorded by Dr. A. R. G. Owen of the Cambridge Psychic Research Society in his book *Can We Explain the Poltergeist?* which was published in 1964. The story begins in 1960 when 11-year-old Virginia Campbell became the center of what seemed to be poltergeist activities. Virginia's father had decided that he and his family should move from Ireland to England. Virginia was sent to stay with her brother and his wife in Sauchie while her father completed his business transactions back in Ireland.

The first signs of trouble in Virginia's temporary home took the form of unexplained raps and thumps that seemed to be coming from the walls of the house. These were followed by the movement of a sideboard, which crept a few inches from a wall and then back again. The Campbells lost no time in calling for help, and the local minister, T. W. Lund, was quick to respond. He reported that he heard loud banging sounds from Virginia's room, coming from a spot near the head of her bed.

MOVING OBJECTS

In 1967 Derek Manning and his wife and three children were living in a relatively new house in Cambridge, England, when they started to hear strange noises in the house. Next, furniture began to shift position and large objects would move or crash to the floor.

The Mannings' son Matthew was 11 years old at the time, and Dr. A. R. G. Owen, a researcher into

Unusual appearance
Objects such as these would suddenly appear and disappear in the Manning household.

things paranormal, informed Matthew's father of the connection between poltergeist activity and adolescents. When the three Manning children were sent to relatives, the PK stopped. However, when Matthew returned home, the activity became even greater than before.

Moving furniture

Matthew described what happened after he went to bed one night : "I suddenly heard a scraping noise coming from the direction of the cupboard. I saw to my horror that the cupboard was inching out from the wall toward me. I felt the bottom end of my bed rising."

The following morning the house was a shambles. As Matthew said: "The dining room looked as though a bomb had hit it. Chairs were upturned and the table was no longer on its feet."

In 1970 the mysterious disturbances stopped as suddenly as they had begun. The Mannings could offer no rational explanation for the disruptions.

A MOTHER'S INFLUENCE

In 1980 staff from the Freiburg (Germany) Institute for Border Areas of Psychology and Mental Hygiene investigated a case in Mulhouse, France. A couple in their mid-thirties lived there with their young son. They had been troubled by apparent poltergeist activity for three years. The researchers found that poltergeist activity only seemed to occur when the mother, who had exhibited psychic tendencies since childhood, was present and they concluded that the activities centered around her.

Hot and cold
Continuous air temperature recordings made during investigation of the Mulhouse case showed inexplicable fluctuations between hot and cold inside the house.

Sudden appearance
According to researchers, a lock of hair and a safety pin suddenly materialized in the basement at Mulhouse.

The poltergeist phenomena were not confined to the Campbell home. Virginia's schoolteacher, Miss Margaret Stewart, remarked that she had seen Virginia frantically holding down the lid of her desk, which seemed to be opening on its own.

In many ways the Sauchie story is typical of many reported poltergeist cases, during which a young person entering puberty is frequently the focus of the disturbances. The child is usually desperately unhappy for one reason or another, and the resultant intense concern might be the trigger that provokes uncontrolled PK.

The Sauchie incident featured inexplicable noises and the levitation of furniture, but some poltergeist cases include different forms of disruption. The following examples are by no means exhaustive but demonstrate the variety of events that can occur during suspected poltergeist activity.

Noisy spirit?

Whatever other phenomena may occur, most poltergeist activity is accompanied by rapping or thumping. Some researchers believe that some form of spirit presence may be responsible for these noises. Such beliefs were especially prevalent in the 19th century.

In 1877 Sir William Barrett, a British physicist and founder of the Society for Psychical Research, investigated suspected poltergeist activity in a house in Derrygonnelly, Ireland. The house was occupied at the time by a widower, his son, and four daughters, aged between 10 and 20. The eldest daughter, Maggie, appeared to be the center of the apparent poltergeist activity, which featured persistent rapping sounds. Sir William accompanied the father and son to the girls' bedroom, where they found Maggie to be the only one awake. Her hands and feet were uncovered.

When the raps began, Sir William lit a gas lamp — and confirmed that no one was moving. There seemed to be no explanation for the sounds.

Stone throwing

Another very common form of poltergeist activity involves the sudden movement of stones. In fact, some of the earliest stories pertaining to poltergeists include tales of rocks being flung with no apparent human involvement. In *Deutsche Mythologie,* published in 1835, writer Jacob Grimm reported a case involving a house in Germany that had been bombarded by stones as far back as A.D. 355. In the 1970's British paranormal researcher Guy Lyon Playfair investigated a number of poltergeist cases in Brazil in conjunction with the Brazilian Institute for Biophysical Research. As Playfair recalls, one family suffered severe damage to their house as a result of rock throwing: "The family had to abandon the house after all the furniture had been damaged by fire and the roof had been pounded to pieces by the furious spirit."

Burning danger

The fact that Playfair's Brazilian case features damage from both rocks and

Hail of stones
Paranormal researcher Guy Lyon Playfair investigates damage to a roof in Brazil.

fire demonstrates how reported poltergeist activity can be more than just a nuisance — it can be dangerous. One of the most spectacular examples of spontaneous fires involved the Willey family of Macomb, Illinois. In August 1948 Mr. Willey, his wife, brother-in-law, eight-year-old nephew, and nine-year-old niece were living in their farmhouse when strange spots began appearing mysteriously on the wallpaper. These spots grew hotter and hotter, then suddenly burst into flames. Pans of water were placed strategically throughout the home, and neighbors trooped in to lend a hand with fighting the recurring fires.

▶ PAGE 140

CASEBOOK

PARKING
PROBLEMS

Without actually acknowledging the existence of the phenomenon, the court's decision did appear to accept the possibility that poltergeists might be real.

WHEN POLTERGEIST STONE-THROWING activity affects the property of a victim's employer, the results are likely to be embarrassing. In the case of Anthony Angelo, the effect was more than just distressing. The poltergeist activity actually managed to land the bewildered employee in court.

In September 1960 Angelo took a job as a handyman at a used car lot in Los Angeles. Soon after, rocks and other objects began flying around. Most apparently traveled horizontally at high speed, causing dents to cars and smashing other property. The objects sometimes seemed to "follow" people and strike them.

The police carried out an intensive investigation and Angelo was arrested as a suspect. It was obvious to most people that the stone throwing occurred only when he was around. Even more suspiciously, all the trouble at the car lot had started on the day that Angelo began to work there.

When Angelo appeared in court, the agency manager, Claude Mock, declared: "I was in the back office sitting on the corner of a desk looking out the back door. The mechanic came in the door and a rock came in at the same time and went out the front door. It came in a straight line. The first day was the worst. The rocks hit every five or ten minutes."

But the manager did not accuse Angelo of throwing the rocks. In fact, Angelo was arrested only after a police captain reportedly said the handyman threw a stone. Yet the captain's testimony in court spoke of Angelo's hitting the side of a car two or three times with his hand. The officer said it was impossible to tell if there was anything in his hand. But a small dent was found in the car door and Angelo was accused of vandalizing the vehicle.

When a police officer was asked in court if he had been able to tell where the stones originated, he replied: "No, sir. During a two-day span we had as many as 30 officers in the field. We couldn't tell where the rocks came from."

The case made headlines in the *Los Angeles Times* on the day after the outbreak began. Among those who attended the trial was a psychical investigator, Raymond Bayless. He made his presence known to the defense attorney and was later called to give evidence. Bayless told the jury about other well-documented cases of stone-throwing poltergeists and compared Angelo's case with these.

Not guilty

Bayless said that although Angelo was responsible for the phenomenon at the car lot, it was possible that the events were being produced paranormally. According to Bayless, Angelo was in one sense just another victim, much as his employer was. The court accepted this explanation, and Angelo was found not guilty. Without actually acknowledging the existence of the phenomenon, the court's decision did appear to accept the possibility that poltergeists might be real.

WORK TROUBLE

When paintings suddenly began rotating almost full circle the investigators finally came to believe that they were out of their depth.

THE CASE OF THE ROSENHEIM poltergeist presents one of the most remarkable instances of possible recurring spontaneous psychokinesis (RSPK) in recent times. And the testimony of 40 reliable witnesses, including police officers and scientists, makes it one of the best documented cases on record.

Sigmund Adam was a lawyer in Rosenheim, a town about 30 miles southwest of Munich. During the summer of 1967, Herr Adam's office phones began developing bizarre problems. Calls were being interrupted, and some were even cut off.

Siemens, the company that had installed the phone system, carried out tests and replaced the receivers and a junction box. This seemed to make no difference. Postal authorities were called in, and they decided to install official phones and a meter to provide a visible record of calls.

Within days, the meter was registering calls when no one was using the phone. Herr Adam discovered that dozens of these calls had been made — all to the service providing the time.

Bizarre happenings

Herr Adam insisted that the post office replace all the telephones and fit the new ones with secure locks. The change made no difference, and the number of calls to the time service increased. But stranger things were about to disrupt the lawyer's office.

On October 20, a loud bang echoed in the office and all the lights went out. According to the electrician who was called in to fix the lights, they had popped when each fluorescent tube had rotated 90° in its socket and disconnected. The electrician replaced the tubes. He had just put his ladder away when there was a second bang and the lights went out again.

The fluorescent tubes were replaced with incandescent bulbs, but these soon began exploding. They had to be covered with nylon bags after a member of staff was injured by flying glass. It was not until November 27, however, when the lights began to swing, that the utility company investigating the phenomena realized that they were dealing with something strange and seemingly inexplicable. At times the swinging would become so violent that the lights would smash against the ceiling.

The office was then disconnected from the main power supply and hooked up to a 7-kilowatt generator parked outside. This made no difference and all the bizarre phenomena continued. When paintings suddenly began rotating almost full circle the investigators finally came to believe that they were out of their depth.

Source of the disturbance

Two of Germany's most eminent physicists, Dr. Friedbert Karger of the Max Planck Institute of Plasma Physics and Dr. G. Zicha of the University of Munich, were called in. Their investigation completed, they speculated that an unknown, complex, and intelligent force that was not electrodynamic was probably responsible for the destruction.

Among the other investigators who visited the office in Rosenheim was a team led by parapsychologist Prof. Hans Bender from the Freiburg Institute for Border Areas of Psychology and Mental Hygiene, which is connected through its library with the University of Freiburg. Using their past experience with poltergeist phenomena, the team came to

theorize that one member of Herr Adam's staff, Annemarie Schneider, was the possible cause of the disturbances. The investigators reportedly noticed that Schneider twitched when odd events occurred, and that when she walked down a corridor the lights would swing.

When Schneider took a week's vacation, the office was peaceful. On her return, light bulbs began exploding, furniture moved, desk drawers opened, and paintings rotated. Eventually, it all became too much for Herr Adam, and in January 1968 Schneider was dismissed and office life returned to normal.

Subconscious fury

When Prof. Bender explained to Schneider that she was causing the strange occurrences, she was bewildered. On the surface she was quiet and well-balanced. However, Prof. Bender felt that underneath Schneider's controlled exterior, her unconscious mind was breaking loose from traumatic oppression, smashing and wrecking anything in sight. The same problem occurred when Schneider took another job. Not surprisingly she was fired again.

When Schneider eventually married and had children in the 1970's, all poltergeist activity stopped. It seemed possible that when she gained emotional stability, the turmoil that she might have been generating finally ended.

SEXUAL CONNECTION

Some researchers, including Prof. Hans Bender of the Freiburg Institute, suggest that poltergeist disturbances result when anxious sexual energy, particularly that which occurs at times of sexual change, is somehow turned outward beyond the confines of the body.

Poltergeist activity often appears to center around people who are going through a time of sexual development, particularly adolescents in puberty, as well as mature women in the years of the menopause, and older men who are experiencing a loss of sexual interest.

Noisy celebration
Poltrabend is a noisy German eve-of-wedding party, during which glasses and crockery are broken to bring the couple luck. The resultant commotion is similiar to that which is associated with poltergeists.

Missing film
Teleportation is a form of PK by which items allegedly pass through solid objects — such as walls and containers. In the Mulhouse, France, poltergeist case, a roll of film reportedly disappeared from inside a sealed camera and was replaced by these drawings

PARANORMAL DRENCHING

In 1963 psychical researcher Raymond Bayless investigated an outbreak of poltergeist activity in the home of the Martin family in Methuen, Massachusetts. The problem began for Francis Martin and his wife and daughter in October of that year when a wet spot suddenly appeared on the wall of their TV room. Then they heard a loud popping sound, and a jet of water shot out from the wall. Within several days there was so much water in the house that the Martin family was forced to move to a relative's apartment.

Water jets

But there was no escape from the deluge. Water began squirting from walls in the relative's home as well. A local fireman could not believe there was a paranormal cause, but testified that he had seen a spray of water break through a plaster wall and jet two feet into the room.

The Martins decided to return to their own home. In an attempt to stop the disruption, the main water supply was shut off. Despite the removal of the source of the water, jets continued to pour from the walls. As with most similar incidents, external action did not diminish the disturbances — they simply had to be allowed to run their course.

Understandably, one of the Willeys' first actions was to call the fire department. The fire officials' initial suggestion was to strip away the wallpaper, yet fires continued to erupt from the bare walls. "The whole thing is so fantastic that I'm almost ashamed to talk about it," the local fire chief told reporters. Within a week, the fires had spread outside to the porch.

In the space of two weeks, fire officials reported that some 200 fires had plagued the family and their home. In the end they lost the fight, and the house was consumed by flames. The Willeys moved into a large tent on their property only to discover that the poltergeist activity was far from over. Besides the tent, two barns and a milkshed on their land burned to the ground, and the family's chicken house was severely damaged.

Curious cascade

Poltergeist activity, however, sometimes centers around water and not fire. In 1972 one such case affected a couple and their 13-year-old daughter, Kerstin, in Scherfede, Germany. Initially, small puddles of water began to form on the floor, followed by the appearance of moist spots on walls and carpets. At the height of this activity, large puddles were appearing on the floor of the living room every 20 minutes — although, according to reports, no one ever saw them form.

Next, floods of water began cascading down stairs. Soon there was too much water to mop up, and so volunteers struggled to brush the water out of the home. The problem lasted for three

days, even after the main water supply to the troubled house had been cut off. Psychic investigators decided that Kerstin was the cause of the problem.

Teleportation

The sudden appearance or disappearance of objects that seem to traverse space and pass through walls, ceilings, and doors often occurs in instances of reported poltergeist activity and is known as teleportation. German psychologist Prof. Hans Bender, head of the Freiburg Institute for Border Areas of Psychology and Mental Hygiene, became a victim of teleportation during a visit to Nickleheim, where he was investigating possible poltergeist disturbances at the home of a laborer, his wife, and their 13-year-old daughter, Brigitte. Having hung his coat in a wardrobe, Prof. Bender was sitting talking to the family, when the mother went to the window to see what was bothering a noisy cat. Prof. Bender was astounded when the woman told him that his coat was out in the snow. Prof. Bender was with the entire family when this happened, and he insisted that no one could have removed the coat without his knowing it. When he retrieved the coat, there appeared to be no footprints in the snow around it.

Other, less well-known, effects associated with poltergeist activity include the appearance of smells, cold spells, voices, and the levitation of objects and people. Occasionally, almost every kind of poltergeist activity has been known to plague households. Yet however disturbing they may be at the time, outbreaks seldom last for more than 18 months.

The main problem for poltergeist investigators is to decide if what happens might be paranormal — or simply produced by hard-to-explain but normal means. In many cases, the researchers suggest that the truth might be a mixture of trickery and possibly genuine psychic energy pulsing out-of-control.

CASEBOOK
RELIABLE WITNESS

"I'm absolutely convinced that no one in the room touched that chair or went anywhere near it when it moved."

*D*URING AN 11-MONTH PERIOD in 1977 and 1978, almost every known form of recurrent spontaneous psychokinesis (RSPK) was recorded at a house in Enfield, on the outskirts of London. The house was occupied by Mrs. Harper and her four children, Janet, Rose, Margaret, and John. The bizarre events began with the appearance of strange shuffling sounds and knockings on walls. Investigators Guy Lyon Playfair and Maurice Grosse from the Society for Psychical Research (SPR) were among those who witnessed many of the 1,500 separate incidents recorded in this case.

The activities seemed to center around 12-year-old Janet. She started to speak in a deep, gruff voice, which claimed to be that of a 72-year-old man who had lived on a nearby street. This "spirit" spoke mainly through Janet and said it was responsible for the strange incidents that were occurring. Both Janet and her sister Margaret were thrown from their beds so frequently that they decided to sleep on the floor. They were also said to have levitated. On one occasion Mrs. Hazel Short, a school-crossing supervisor, said she saw Janet and various objects floating around the room, striking the window frame on each circuit. Other phenomena recorded by Playfair and Grosse included cutlery bending before witnesses, drawers opening and closing in unison, large items of furniture moving, and paper and cloth catching fire spontaneously.

Within days of the outbreak, two police officers were called to the house. They were among the surprised witnesses to the sudden movement of a chair. Carolyn Heeps, a police constable, gave this testimony: "The chair was by the sofa. I looked at the chair and noticed that it shook slightly. I can't explain it any better. It came off the floor nearly a half-inch. I saw it slide off to the right about three and a half to four feet before it came to rest. I'm absolutely convinced that no one in the room touched that chair or went anywhere near it when it moved."

Playing games

For the most part, the sophisticated technology of the 20th century was no match for the apparent cunning of the Enfield poltergeist. Playfair and Grosse hoped that the use of video cameras and other equipment would result in conclusive proof that the mayhem had no rational cause. Instead, the equipment continually broke down, behaved erratically, or simply would not work. It was as if the PK forces were playing games with the researchers.

Playfair and Grosse were satisfied that what they and others had witnessed constituted genuine paranormal events. In 1978 a heated debate followed the presentation of their findings at the SPR's International Conference in Cambridge, England, when other SPR members said the two men had been taken in by the children. The Enfield poltergeist case became a classic struggle between cynics who blamed mischievous girls and believers who thought something more significant was happening.

INDEX

Page numbers in **bold** type refer to illustrations and captions.

PHOTOGRAPHIC SOURCES

John Beckett: 79t, 94br, 109b, 114l, 119tc, 123br, 131l, r; **Biofotos**/Heather Angel: 96c; **Biophoto Associates**: 45; **Bodleian Library**/John Johnson Collection: 36t; **Bridgeman Art Library**: 23l (Giraudon), 27 (Giraudon), 32b (Smithsonian Institute), 40tr, 65t (Corcoran Gallery), 79b (British Museum); **Stephen H. Brooks**: 59r; **Jean-Loup Charmet**: 29r, 40br, 41t, 42c, b, 43br, 63b, 94bl, 109tr, 134l; **Bruce Coleman Ltd.**: 55r (M. Berge); **Colorific**: 125br (C. Callis); **Robert Cracknell**: 100t; **John Cutten**: 65b, 119cr, br; **Dr. Jule Eisenbud**, Psycho-Physical Research Foundation: 119cl; **Mrs. J.N. Emerson**: 102l; **English Heritage**: 125t; **The Milton H. Erickson Foundation**: 47t; **Mary Evans Picture Library**: 41c, b, 42t (Explorer), 43l, 46t (Sigmund Freud Copyrights), 50t, b, 51t, c, 53t, b, 56t, 58bl, 59l, 70l, 71l, 78l, 80t, 83t (Society for Psychical Research), b, 90l, 92b, 93b, 106tr (M. Cassirer), 107br, 113tl, 120l, 121t, b, 122t, cl (G. Playfair), br, 124l, 125cr, 136r (G. Playfair); **Express Newspapers**, London: 130r; *Fate Magazine*, Nov. 1979 (story & pictures): 99l; **Fortean Picture Library**: 80b (Dr. E.R. Gruber), 93cr, 97c, 102cr (Gruber), 106cr & br (Gruber), 107tl (Dr. J.T. Richards), bl (Gruber), 109c (D. Stacey), 118t, b (Richards), 122cr (Richards), 123t (Dr. B.E. Schwarz), cl & c (Dr. J. Thomas), cr (Gruber), bl (Richards), 124c, 125bl (Richards), 129t, 136tl & bl (Gruber), 140t (Gruber); **Foundation for Research on the Nature of Man**, Durham, NC: 81t, b, 110l, 112r, 114r; **Leif Geiges**: 84, 101t, 116tl, bl, br; **Uri Geller**: 128t, b, 130l, 132t, b, 133t, b; **John Glover**: 96tl; **Henry Gris**: 76, 85t, b; **Dr. E.R. Gruber**: 115t, b; **Dr. Howard R. Hall**/Colin Klein: 48b; **Hella Hammid**: 82; **Hulton Picture Co.**: 31, 64b (E. Auerbach), 67 (Keystone), 69t, 73r, 93cl, 102br; **Hutchison Library**: 32t, 33l (J. Wright), 72bl (L. Taylor); **Images Colour Library**/Charles Walker Collection: 28l, 35t, 92t, 97br, 103t, 118c; **Imperial War Museum**: 29bl, 92c; from *The Margins of Reality: The Role of Consciousness in the Physical World* by Robert J. Jahn & Brenda J. Dunne, Harcourt Brace Jovanovich, 1987: 113tr; **Kinema Collection**: 52, 58tr; **Kobal Collection**: 58br; available through **Leading Edge Retail Ltd.**: 57cr;

Mrs. M. Lethbridge: 96tr; **Mansell Collection**: 62r, 94t; **Ginette Matacia**/Olan Mills, Chattanooga, TN: 99r; **Louis & Ginette Matacia**, Alexandria, VA: 91l, r; **NASA**: 129b; **Natural History Photographic Agency**: 20l (S.Dalton); **Novosti**: 37b, 47b; **Oxford Scientific Films**: 36cl (K.Day); **Popperfoto**: 28r, 69b, 70r, 100b, 101c, 107tr, 108t; **Psychic Press**: 122bl; **Dr. Martin Reiser**, LAPD: 57cl; **Rex Features**: 51bl & br (SIPA/Mechain), 55l (J.Hasenkopf), 57t, b, 119tr; **Science Photo Library**: 21l & r (G.Hadjo/CNRI), 23r (A.Pasieka), 25t (J.Mazziotta), b (US Dept. of Energy), 40l (D.Parker), 64c (B.Blass), 90r, 108-9 background (P.Loiez), 108bl & br (P.Loiez), 109tl (Lawrence Berkeley Lab.); **Brian Snellgrove**: 135r; **Dr. Roger Sperry**: 26t; **Frank Spooner Pictures/Gamma**: 24b (Liaison), 29tl, 36b, 43tr (Novosti), 56b (Milosh), 63t (Magniez), 64t (Hemsey), 71r (Jahiel), 103b (APN); **Syndication International**: 58tl, 119bl (Dr. Jule Eisenbud), 129c; **Topham Picture Source**: 46b (A.Purkiss), 97bl; **Touro Infirmary**, New Orleans, LA: 48t; **David Towersey**: 24t, 33r; **UPI/Bettmann**: 53c, 62l, 101b; **Dr. Jan Merta de Velehrad**: 97t; **Zefa**: 26b (Craddock), 34t (D.Baglin), b (P.W.Fera), 35b, 36cr (Dr.F.Sauer), 37t (McAllister), cr (Spoenlein), 72t (E.Mathe), 93t (K.Kummels), 94c (G.Heil), 96-7 background, 96bl, br.

b - bottom; c - center; t - top; r - right; l - left.

Efforts have been made to contact the holder of the copyright for each picture. In several cases these have been untraceable, for which we offer our apologies.